CROSSINGS

by

Clare Duffy

CW00972903

Actors:

Adam	Paul Amos
Rob	Jem Dobbs
Bethan	Eiry Hughes
Jane	Michelle Luther
Stephen	Jamie Newall
Ruth	Clêr Stephens
Sam	Dylan Williams

Director:	Simon Harris
Designer:	David Farley
Lighting Designer:	Guy Hoare

Stage Manager:	Richard Balshaw
Production Manager:	Sarah Cole
Technical Stage Manager:	Elanor Higgins
Technical Assistant:	Dom Bilkey
Costume Assistant:	Kate Bohin
Assistant Director:	Alex Ferris

Note: Text was correct at time of going to press,
but may have changed during rehearsal.

sgriptcymru
contemporarydramawales

sgriptcymru is the national company for contemporary drama in Wales, specialising in new writing by Welsh and Wales-based playwrights.

The company holds a pivotal role in discovering and promoting exciting new voices for the stage. **sgript**cymru is unique in its exclusive dedication to producing new writing in both Welsh and English. It is also a development organisation that works with emerging playwrights at the grass roots level, as well as a commissioning company working with professional playwrights and offering rare freedom to their creativity.

Through **sgript**cymru's professional support to dramatists and its award-winning programme of new productions each year, the company aims to ensure the continuing existence of a new writing culture in Wales and to enhance its place in the wider world. The company has gained an enviable reputation for the quality and range of its work in theatres nationwide since its inception in 2000.

"The excellent new writing company"
The Guardian, June 2003

The Company:

Artistic Director	Simon Harris
Associate Director	Elen Bowman
Administrative Director	Mai Jones
Development Director	Emma Routledge
Literary Manager	Angharad Elen
Marketing Manager	Siân Melangell Dafydd
Administrative Officer	Steffan Cravos
Artistic Associate	Bethan Jones
Associate Writer	Meic Povey

The Board of Directors:

Ann Beynon (Chair), Frances Medley (Vice-Chair), Philippa Davies, Nicola Heywood-Thomas, Richard Houdmont, Elwyn Tudno Jones, David Seligman, Lucy Shorrocks, Hedd Vine, Elinor Williams, Mared Hughes (Associate Member).

CROSSINGS

Clare Duffy

ISBN: 0–9543710-6-2

For permission to perform one of the plays published here, contact:
sgriptcymru, Chapter, Market Road, Canton, Cardiff, CF5 1QE.

Tel: 029 2023 6650
sgriptcymru@sgriptcymru.com
www.sgriptcymru.com

This play was commissioned by **sgript**cymru and first performed by the company on 9 March 2005 in Chapter Arts Centre, Cardiff.

CEFNOGI CREADIGRWYDD
CYNGOR CELFYDDYDAU CYMRU
THE ARTS COUNCIL OF WALES
SUPPORTING CREATIVITY

Esmée
Fairbairn
FOUNDATION

This book is published with the financial support of the Welsh Books Council.

Cover design and image: A1
Typesetting: Eira Fenn
Printed in Wales by Cambrian Printers, Aberystwyth

Cyhoeddiadau Dalier Sylw

sgriptcymru Publications

Available from:

sgriptcymru
Chapter, Market Road, Canton, Cardiff, CF5 1QE
Tel: 029 2023 6650
sgriptcymru@sgriptcymru.com
www.sgriptcymru.com

Playwright: Clare Duffy

Having graduated from the University of Leeds with a degree in English and Theatre Studies, Clare went on to co-found Unlimited Theatre in 1997 with five other Leeds students. She completed her MA in Scriptwriting at the University of Glamorgan in 2002. She was Community Writer for **sgript**cymru in 2001, developing new writing in Swansea and Carmarthenshire. In 2003, Clare received the Pearson Award, which supported the commission of *A Good Man* and enabled a year-long residency with the West Yorkshire Playhouse.

Director: Simon Harris

Simon Harris is Artistic Director of **sgript**cymru and *Crossings* will be his fifth production for the company. Born and brought up in Swansea, Simon studied English at University College, London and trained as an actor at RADA. He founded Thin Language Theatre Company in 1992, directing *Forever Yours Marie Lou* and *Nothing To Pay* for the company, the last being his adaptation of the novel by Caradoc Evans. Other directorial work includes *The Dresser* at Plymouth Theatre Royal. As a writer, his first play, *Badfinger*, premiered at The Donmar Warehouse and as a result Simon was nominated Most Promising Playwright in the 1997 Evening Standard Drama Awards. He has also written *Wales>Alaska* for the Royal National Theatre, *Garageland* for Steel Wasps and *Milk and Honey* for Soho Theatre Company. His previous productions for **sgript**cymru include *Franco's Bastard* by Dic Edwards (Best New Play in the Theatre in Wales Awards 2002), *past away* by Tracy Harris and *Indian Country* by Meic Povey, which opened at Chapter Arts Centre, Cardiff before touring Wales and also being staged at the Traverse Theatre in Edinburgh. Most recently, Simon has directed Gary Owen's *Ghost City*, which enjoyed successful tours of Wales and England before receiving acclaim in New York and London.

Paul Amos (Adam)

Paul is originally from the rugby hotbed of Pencoed. He was educated at Ysgol Gyfun Llanhari where he discovered his love for acting. Paul further developed his acting at the National Youth Theatre of Great Britain, Cardiff's Everyman Theatre Festival and at LAMDA for three years.

Since graduating, Paul has appeared in a six-month tour with the RSC in *The Duchess of Malfi*, directed by Gayle Edwards; has played the lead in *Blood and Roses*, directed by Toby Wiltshire, with Trestle Theatre (sold-out Edinburgh Festival and UK tour); and has also appeared in *The Shadow of a Boy* (NT Studio). Paul is a founding member of Faction Theatre Company, whose first production, *The War is Dead Long Live the War*, toured Wales and London to great acclaim.

Paul's television credits include *Casualty*, *Signs of Life* and *Jacob's Ladder*. Most recently, Paul has relocated from London to Toronto to be with his girlfriend and to pursue an acting career in Canada. Paul is very pleased to be returning to Wales to work with such an innovative and vital company, and just in time for Wales's Six Nations campaign!

Jem Dobbs (Rob)

Since graduating from Bretton Hall, Jem's credits include: *Threepenny Opera* for Theatre Workshop at Festival Theatre, Edinburgh; actor and musician in *Buddy Bolden Experience*, directed by Garry Robson, commissioned by the Royal Exchange, Manchester, and performed at the Royal Exchange and the Edinburgh Fringe; Minstrel in *Carnival Messiah* at the West Yorkshire Playhouse, directed by Geraldine Connor; Assistant Music Director and character of mad priest Folio in an adaptation of the *Hunchback of Notre Dame* in Shrewsbury Castle, directed by Garry Robson; Feste in *Twelfth Night* for Theatre of the Dales Touring Company, directed by Dave Robertson; 274 in *Victoria Station* (Pinter) at West Yorkshire Playhouse; and Prospero in a radical adaptation of *The Tempest* touring the UK for six months. Jem also plays the trumpet and vocals for various Leeds bands. *Crossings* marks Jem's debut with **sgript**cymru.

Eiry Hughes (Bethan)

Eiry Hughes trained in East 15 Acting School. Her theatre work includes Ruby in *Buzz* for **sgript**cymru, Lynne in *A Difference Between Friends* (tour) for Paradoxis Productions and Mathilda in *Zastrozzi* at Barons Court Theatre for Up and Out Productions.
Her television credits include Stacey in *Belonging* (BBC Wales), Ann in *Emyn Roc a Rôl* (S4C) and Clare in *A470* (HTV).
Her latest short films include Carol in *Still Living* for Black Rose Productions and Maggie in *Hope Help* for The Lagrangian Points.

Michelle Luther (Jane)

Since graduating from the Royal Welsh College of Music and Drama Michelle's theatre credits include: *And Now What*, *The Crucible*, *The Ballad of Megan Morgan* (Clwyd Theatr Cymru), *Scotland Road* (EYE Theatre) and *Hamlet H2O* (ELAN Wales).

Her television credits include: *Tracy Beaker 'The Movie of Me'* (BBC), *Danielle Cable: Eye Witness* (GRANADA), *Eastenders* (BBC), *The Bench* (BBC) and *Tales of Pleasure Beach* (BLAST! Films).

Jamie Newall (Stephen)

Jamie was born in Edinburgh and trained at the Bristol Old Vic Theatre School. His repertory work includes appearances at Harrogate, Coventry, Salisbury, Edinburgh, Sheffield, Nottingham, Birmingham, Watford, Stoke and Manchester: *Winter's Tale* (Leontes), *Hay Fever* (Simon), *The Duchess Of Malfi* (Antonio), *Shadow Of A Gunman* (Davoren), *Mary Rose* (Simon), *Hobson's Choice* (Willie Mossop), *Cherry Orchard* (Trofimov), *Britannicus* (Nero), *Dr Faustus* (title role), *Volpone* (Corvino), *The Atheist's Tragedy* (Languebeau Snuffe), *Kind Hearts and Coronets* (all the d'Ascoynes), *Neville's Island* (Roy), *Twelfth Night* (Aguecheek) and *Waters Of the Moon* (Julius Winterhalter). His work in London and abroad includes: Judd in *Another Country* (Queen's Theatre); *Richard III, Henry V, Hamlet, Red Noses, A Christmas Carol* (RSC); Time Out Award for Nathan Leopold in *Never The Sinner* (Offstage); *The Great Pretenders*, Robespierre in *Danton's Death* (Gate); Abel Drugger in *The Alchemist* (RNT); The Actor in *The Woman in Black* (Fortune Theatre); Osric in *Hamlet* (Elsinore); Don Pedro/Friar/Ursula in *Much Ado About Nothing* (AFTLS); Castel in *The Tunnel* (Croydon Warehouse and Edinburgh Festival).

His TV credits include: *Trelawny of the Wells*; *Yes, Prime Minister*; *Devices and Desires*; *Sex, Guys and Videotape*; *Casualty* and *The Bill*. His radio work includes: *Friends Of Oscar, Baltasar and Blimunda, The Mouse that Roared, Colonel Warburton's Madness, McClevy* and *Flashman*.

Clêr Stephens (Ruth)

Clêr Stephens, originally from Bargoed, south Wales, trained in Edinburgh. She has worked most recently with Unnos Productions in a short film, *Amser Chwarae/ Playtime*, which premiered at the Cardiff International Film Festival 2004.

Her various theatre credits include Mappa Mundi's Constance in *The Three Musketeers*, Viola in *Twelfth Night* and Audrey in *As You Like It*. She has worked with Theatr na n'Óg, Hijinx, Spectacle, Medium Rare, Galloglass and Theatre West Glamorgan.

Most recently she has worked with Clwyd Theatr Cymru, Gwent Theatre, Rachel Calder Productions and Theatr Gargaphie on *The Divine Caligula*. Rehearsed readings have taken her to Stockholm for Theatre Royal Plymouth with Peter G. Morgan's *Special*, Royal Court Theatre with Jenny Livsey's *A Face Like Robert Redford* and Soho Theatre with Sally Ann Gritton's *Sorted Symposium* and *Sorted Symposium 2*.

Clêr has worked several times for Radio 4 including *Leaving This Land* by Emma Reeves and *A Letter From A Far Country* by Gillian Clarke. She has also worked for RTE on *Breathing Space* by Ken Bourke.

Her TV credits include various BBC, S4C and HTV productions, among them *A Mind To Kill*, *Pobol y Cwm* and *Gary Phelps*.

Dylan Williams (Sam)

Dylan graduated from the Royal Welsh College of Music and Drama in 2002. Since then he has worked extensively with the New Victoria Theatre, Stoke where he most recently played the role of Gerald in Oscar Wilde's *A Woman of No Importance*. Other work for the New Vic includes *Amadeus* and two operas, *Carmen* and *The Marriage of Figaro*, which toured to the Bolton Octagon Theatre and the Stephen Joseph Theatre, Scarborough.

Other theatre work includes: *Oh What a Lovely War* (Clwyd Theatr Cymru); *Sleeping Beauty* and *Aladdin* (Everyman Theatre, Cheltenham); *You're Not Singing Any More* (Show of Strength Theatre Company) and *Panto* (Cwmni Mega).

He has also worked as a performer and facilitator for European Live Art Network/ ELAN Wales and has been involved in nearly a dozen site-specific devised projects in Wales and Italy. Further projects include: *Vera* (ELAN – Reykjavik); *Maskinen* (ELAN – Denmark) and *Woyzeck* (ELAN – tour of India).

His television appearances include *A470* (ITV Wales) and his radio and voice-over work includes: *The Snow Spider* (BBC Radio 4/Radio 7); *The Small Mine* (BBC Radio 4); *Dani* and *Twrw* (BBC Radio Cymru); *Jibba Jabba*, *Traed Moch* and *Medabots* (Atsain for S4C); *Under Milk Wood* (Royal Welsh College of Music and Drama) and *Beatrix Potter Tales* (Sain for S4C).

Dylan was also a member of the National Youth Theatre of Wales and was involved in productions of *Faust* and *Hamlet* (playing Hamlet).

Designer: David Farley

David Farley graduated from Wimbledon School of Art in 1999.

His recent design work includes *The Lemon Princess*, directed by Ruth Carney (West Yorkshire Theatre); *The Little Fir Tree*, written and directed by James Philips (Crucible Studio Theatre, Sheffield); *Zero Degrees and Drifting*, devised with Unlimited Theatre (touring); *Quartermaine's Terms*, directed by Simon Godwin (Theatre Royal, Northampton and Salisbury Playhouse); *Could It Be Magic*, devised with Unlimited Theatre (Crucible Studio Theatre, Sheffield); *Macbeth*, adapted and directed by James Philips (Crucible Studio Theatre, Sheffield); *Observe the Sons of Ulster Marching Towards the Somme*, directed by James Philips (Jericho Productions at The Pleasance, London); *The Seagull*, directed by Simon Godwin (Theatre Royal, Northampton); *Dealer's Choice*, directed by Angus Jackson (Clwyd Theatr Cymru); *Sexual Perversity in Chicago* and *The Shawl*, directed by Angus Jackson (Crucible Theatre, Sheffield); *Pink Orthodox* (Shunt at Riverside Studios); *Works on Canvas* and *Here Lie Hedwig and Stoller* (Shunt at the Arch, Bethnal Green); *The Dybbuk*, directed by Mark Rosenblatt, James Menzies-Kitchen Memorial Trust Award (Battersea Arts Centre); *Someone Who'll Watch Over Me*, directed by Mark Rosenblatt (Burton-Taylor Theatre, Oxford).

Lighting Designer: Guy Hoare

Guy is a freelance lighting designer based in London. He has previously worked with Clare Duffy on Unlimited Theatre's *Could It Be Magic?* and *Zero Degrees and Drifting*, both of which were designed by David Farley. He has also lit David's designs for *The Little Fir Tree* and *Macbeth* in Sheffield and *Observe the Sons of Ulster Marching Towards the Somme* in London. Other recent designs for theatre include Caryl Churchill's *Fen* and *Far Away* in Sheffield, Joe Penhall's *Love and Understanding* in London, *The Ballad of Johnny 5 Star* at the Library in Manchester and *The Caretaker* for London Classic Theatre Company, for whom he has been the resident designer for the last five years. Much of Guy's recent work has been in contemporary dance. He has been the lighting designer for the award-winning Henri Oguike Dance Company since 2000 and has just completed tours of Europe and the Middle East with them. He has also collaborated with Shobana Jeyasingh, Maresa von Stockert, Igloo, The Snag Project and The Mark Bruce Company. Last summer, he revived his designs for Wagner's *Ring Cycle* at Longborough Festival Opera, where in recent years he has also lit productions of *Tosca* and *The Magic Flute*.

In London he has designed *Cinderella* (for the Royal Opera House Education Department) and several operas at the Hackney Empire and BAC. He has also designed lighting for classical music concerts at the Purcell Room for Pedro Carneiro, the Arditti Quartet and the Nash Ensemble.

Stage Manager: Richard Balshaw

Since graduating from the Welsh College of Music and Drama in 1999, Richard has worked for many theatre companies in Wales and England as Production/ Stage Manager, as well as being a technical director at a performing arts training centre in New York.

Richard has also production/stage managed various television and music events for companies such as Radio 1, MTV, Emap, *Q* and *Kerrang Magazine*. He has spent the past eleven months touring around Europe and Scandinavia with RIVERDANCE Avoca Company as part of the production team. *Crossings* will be Richard's first show with **sgript**cymru and he is looking forward to the challenge and being back out on the road touring.

Production Manager: Sarah Cole

Having spent the last ten years working professionally in Wales, Sarah now works freelance, specialising in production and site management both for theatre and outdoor events.

Over the last two years she has worked for the Welsh College of Music and Drama, Clear Channel Entertainment, SJM, Wales Theatre Company, Freshwater UK and Cardiff County Council.

Sarah was Production Manager for the outdoor celebrations of the opening of the Wales Millennium Centre in November 2004.

She is the Chair of Cardiff – Wales Lesbian and Gay Mardi Gras, Chair of the Theatr Iolo Board and a co-opted member on the Stonewall Cymru Exec.

Technical Stage Manager: Elanor Higgins

Elanor is a graduate of the Royal Welsh College of Music and Drama where she now works part-time as a lecturer in lighting design.

A freelance lighting designer herself, she has lit ten previous productios for **sgript**cymru, the most recent being *Drws Arall i'r Coed* in February 2005. Other lighting designs include *The Caretaker* for The Torch Theatre, *Erogenous Zones* for The Sherman Theatre and *Rats, Buckets and Bombs* for The Nottingham Playhouse.

Before becoming a freelance lighting designer she worked as a full-time lighting technician for Welsh National Opera, The Royal National Theatre and Leicester Haymarket. She has just returned from a year travelling abroad with her husband.

Technical Assistant: Dom Bilkey

Dom was born and brought up in Cornwall and discovered a passion for theatre at an early age. After starting out in village pantomime he eventually decided that theatre was the career to pursue.

He attended the Royal Welsh College of Music and Drama in Cardiff and after graduating in 2004 started his professional career as Stage Manager for Theatr na n'Óg (*Big Bad Wolf*). His other work includes Sound Operator (*Tristan and Yseult*) and Technical Stage Manager (*The Bacchae*), both for Kneehigh Theatre. He also has sound design credits for Kneehigh Theatre (*Wagstaffe The Wind-up Boy*) and New Theatre Works (*Carry On Down The River*).

This is his first time working with **sgript**cymru.

Costume Assistant: Kate Bohin

Kate is a recent graduate of the Royal Welsh College of Music and Drama where she graduated with a 2:1 Honours Degree in Theatre Design, and she is now working as a freelance costume maker. Her most recent work has been making costumes for *Treflan*, a Welsh-language production for S4C. She has also worked on *Santa's Missing Trousers*, a pantomine in Milford Haven and she is currently working for the Welsh National Youth Opera as the wardrobe supervisor.

Assistant Director: Alex Ferris

Since graduating from Liverpool John Moores University in 2001, Alexander's involvement in theatre has been varied: from working as stage crew to leading workshops and from administration to directing productions.

His recent directing experience includes *Meat* by Owen Thomas (nominated for a Theatre in Wales award) and assisting Jeff Teare for Made in Wales's production of *Football* by Lewis Davies, which premiered at the Edinburgh Fringe 2004. Alexander is also currently directing a piece for the Sherman Youth Theatre's *Interiors* project and in February 2005 he will relaunch *UnZipped* at the Sherman Theatre, Cardiff – a scheme he set up to showcase the work of young writers, actors and directors. As a young director himself, Alexander is very pleased to be working and learning with **sgript**cymru.

CROSSINGS

by CLARE DUFFY

Characters:

        Adam
        Rob
        Bethan
        Jane
        Stephen
        Ruth
        Sam

ACT I

SCENE 1

*A young male figure is face down on the ground as if fallen. He turns and lies straight as a corpse. **Jane**, a 17 year old girl, is pulling her shirtsleeves over the bandages around her wrists.*

RUTH: (*Unseen*) It's the phone for you. It's Bethan. Again.

JANE: I'm not in.

*She has just covered the bandages as **Ruth**, a 38 year old woman enters.*

RUTH: I don't like lying, Jane.

JANE: Really.

RUTH: She's on her way over.

JANE: I'm tired.

RUTH: Shouldn't 've stayed out all night then, should you? Where did you stay?

JANE: A friend's.

RUTH: You can lie to her yourself, can't you?

JANE: Whatever.

Ruth exits.

A male figure, around 16 years old is now standing calmly.

SAM:	I'm dead.
JANE:	I know, dumb ass.
SAM:	Still hot though.
JANE:	You stink.
SAM:	What, worse than normal?
JANE:	No, s'pose not.
SAM:	Bet you never thought you'd see me again.
JANE:	No, s'pose not.
SAM:	Nice send-off.
JANE:	Sorry?
SAM:	No . . . thanks. Nice of you to be there.
JANE:	Didn't know.
SAM:	Really?
JANE:	I didn't.
	Not 'til yesterday . . . too late to go.
	I couldn't.
SAM:	Excuses, excuses. I've been the talk of the town. The tragedy queens have been having a ball!

JANE:	Only found out yesterday. Honest. No time. Feel like shit and . . .
SAM:	Tune?
JANE:	What you want?
SAM:	Pop-whore trash.

She puts on the music.

JANE:	There you go.
SAM:	You've got this?
JANE:	It's yours.
SAM:	Tea leaf!
JANE:	Got to sleep.
SAM:	Don't . . . listen . . . (*They listen to the music. Jane looks at Sam.*)
	I wanted this, at my funeral. I wanted something like this.
	Not that God shit.
	Being dead is, like, so Sidcup!
JANE:	Oh, Sam.
SAM:	I might not 've been found for fousands of years. Bodies are found in bogs sometimes with all their teeth and everything. I could have been a fabulous mystery mud man.

JANE: Am I asleep?

SAM: No.

JANE: What do you want?

SAM: I was in the mud, in the water, a long time.

JANE: What are you doing here?

SAM: Went west.

JANE: West?

SAM: West.

JANE: It's not true.

            It's still not true. Can't believe you're . . .

SAM: Believe it, baby.

JANE: Is that why you're here? Because I can't believe you're . . .

SAM: Shut up!

            I want you to do something for me.

JANE: What?

SAM: It wasn't an accident.

JANE: What?

SAM: I was killed.

*He reaches around for the knife that is hidden under **Jane**'s bed.*

SAM: Left on the mud and sand.

JANE: No.

SAM: Yes.

JANE: You're not . . . just saying that?

SAM: Why would I? Got nothing to gain now.

JANE: No. Fuck. Lies.

SAM: Everyone thinks I topped meself. I know.

JANE: They said it was an accident.

SAM: Yeah, but that's just so no one has to feel too guilty.

JANE: But who? How?

SAM: You'll find out.

There's a knock at the door.

SAM: For me.

BETHAN: (*From outside*) Jane? Jane, can I come in?

SAM: See ya.

*He rolls himself up in a sheet from **Jane**'s bed.*

JANE: When?

Bethan, a 17 year old girl enters. She's wearing funeral clothes.

BETHAN: Is this place ever going to be finished? Those builders are
            really doing my head in.

JANE: Bethan!

BETHAN: They're taking the fucking piss.

JANE: Don't take any notice.

BETHAN: Is your phone off?

JANE: Dunno . . . yes.

BETHAN: What's wrong?

JANE: Nothing . . . why?

BETHAN: You're fucking pale.

JANE: I'm fine.

BETHAN: Jane, for fuck's sake.

JANE: What?

BETHAN: You're bleeding.

Jane unwraps and rewraps her bandages on one wrist.

BETHAN: I called you all last night and this morning.

JANE: I'm fine.

BETHAN: I wanted to say sorry.

JANE:	Whatever.
BETHAN:	Don't be like that.
	I know I lost it, OK. I lost my temper. I'm sorry.
JANE:	OK.
BETHAN:	You didn't have to run off.

*Silence from **Jane** as she finishes wrapping her arm.*

BETHAN:	Why do you . . .?
JANE:	What?
BETHAN:	It looks fucking painful.

***Bethan** moves towards **Jane** and reaches out for her arms.*

BETHAN:	Where did you go?
JANE:	A and E.
BETHAN:	Why?
JANE:	I had an accident; it was an emergency.
BETHAN:	You said you weren't going to do it again. They look way harsh.
JANE:	I'm harsh.
BETHAN:	Least you had them cleaned properly.

*Jane grunts in an 'I don't know why I bothered' way. **Bethan** picks up the knife that **Sam** was holding.*

BETHAN: You were going to throw this away.

JANE: It was a present from Sam.

BETHAN: (*Hides the knife back under the bed*) I kept trying your mobile.

JANE: There wasn't any point talking.

BETHAN: No?

   You're not the only one.

JANE: What?

BETHAN: I knew him too.

JANE: No, it's different. We had a special . . . he was my best friend.

BETHAN: Then why wouldn't you go to his funeral?

JANE: Don't start that again.

BETHAN: You make me so fucking angry.

JANE: You gonna dump me then?

BETHAN: Do you want me to?

JANE: Yes . . .

BETHAN: Don't believe you.

JANE: Good.

BETHAN: You should have been there. (*She starts to cry*) I still can't
                   believe it.

*She reaches out for **Jane** and pulls her in, hugging her tightly. She then*
*pulls away, just enough to kiss **Jane**.*

JANE: No.

BETHAN: What?

JANE: I just can't.

BETHAN: You don't love me any more?

JANE: I do. I just can't.

***Jane** kisses her quickly.*

JANE: There. Don't leave. OK? I just can't touch anyone, OK?

BETHAN: God, you're so cold!

She pulls a blanket from the bed around her shoulders. They sit on the
end of the bed together.

JANE: That's a dress.

BETHAN: You like?

JANE: I do. You look beautiful.

BETHAN: Really?

JANE: How was it?

BETHAN:	Short, sad.
JANE:	Mum was nagging me about going.
BETHAN:	You should've.
JANE:	Don't start.
BETHAN:	Sorry.
JANE:	'An, I don't think it was an accident.
BETHAN:	What do you mean?
JANE:	Do you believe in ghosts?
BETHAN:	Don't think so.
JANE:	Do you think that if you really thought really hard about someone who'd died, who you loved, they would come to you?

Or if they needed you to do something for them, they would come to you? |
| BETHAN: | You might want that so much you could believe that they'd come to you.

I know you miss him. But he's dead. He can't come back. |
JANE:	But it was weird, wasn't it?
BETHAN:	What?
JANE:	The way he . . . went.

BETHAN: Why?

JANE: Can you keep a secret?

BETHAN: What?

JANE: Sam was murdered.

BETHAN: No!

JANE: Think about it. What was he doing out in Llanelli? Normally he'd be going out in Cardiff on a Saturday night.

BETHAN: Maybe he met someone.

JANE: Exactly. Met someone. How else did he get so far out there on the mud banks?

BETHAN: Don't know. But I don't think . . .

Jane kisses her.

JANE: Do you love me?

BETHAN: Yes.

JANE: Would do anything for me?

BETHAN: Kiss me again.

JANE: (*Jane kisses her*) Would you make hot water bottles for me and stand up for me and . . . take me to the sea and help me find out who killed our friend Sam?

BETHAN: I don't think . . .

JANE: Where does the river meet the sea?

BETHAN: The mouth.

Jane kisses Bethan and they fall back on the bed wrapped up in the blanket and each other.

SAM: (*Holding the knife again*) From the bank the water looks grey. In the estuary it's grey. Mud on the bank, like cake mixture, but it's still grey.

               Not what I meant.

               No escape.

               Didn't want grey.

               I'm bored. Seagulls crap on you. Tide is . . . repetitive.

JANE: Shit! Stop. (*She is shaking*)

BETHAN: What's wrong? For fuck's sake.

JANE: I just can't.

BETHAN: Fine.

JANE: I'm sorry.

BETHAN: What?

JANE: I can't explain.

BETHAN: You scared you'll enjoy yourself?

               That you might actually have some fun?

BETHAN (con.): . . .

I've got to go.

I've got homework to do . . . so have you.

JANE: Yeah.

BETHAN: Do you really want to go there?

JANE: Yes.

BETHAN: I'll come with you if you want.

JANE: I don't want to go really.

BETHAN: Sure you do. You can be Willow and I'll be Tara.

JANE: 'Always making with the funny!'

BETHAN: See you tomorrow, yeah?

JANE: Yeah.

BETHAN: Get some sleep.

Bethan leaves.

SAM: You're such a lucky bitch.

JANE: Perv.

SAM: She's all over you like a sticky rash.

JANE: So?

SAM: 'I can't', 'I can't' . . . you can't feel more alive than that. Shouldn't give that up for anybody!

JANE: I don't do 'Life'.

SAM: Get the git what done this to me! Please.

JANE: How?

SAM: I don't know. Go to where I was found. Look for clues. Ask questions. Find out who did this to me. They're out there, alive, and I'm here and dead.

JANE: I can't.

SAM: (*He puts the knife in her hand*) Go where they found me.

JANE: No. I'm not feeling well.

RUTH: (*Shouting from downstairs*) Jane!

SAM: They're getting away with it. I'm sixteen and I'm fucking grey.

RUTH: (*From just outside the door*) Jane.

SAM: See ya, wouldn't wanna . . .

Sam picks up the sheet and wraps it around himself then lies down again.

RUTH: (*Entering*) Jane, I've been calling you. Why didn't you answer?

JANE: Must 've been sleeping.

Ruth looks around at the mess of books; she picks up the sheet around **Sam**, he shivers.

RUTH: Did you have a nice time with Bethan?

Sam snorts. *Jane* mumbles something like, '*I suppose*'.

RUTH: We could do with giving this place a good spring-clean.

JANE: Oh god, Mum!

           I know where everything is.

RUTH: (*She picks up a few books and inspects them*) Why don't
           you read something decent?

JANE: Mum!

RUTH: Filling your head with all these detective stories! Murder
           mysteries!

           Did you read that Jeanette Winterson I gave you? Her
           mum was a real cow. You don't know how lucky you are.

           You don't . . .

JANE: Shut up, Mum.

RUTH: Jane!

           (*Regains her temper*) I need to talk to you.

           No, I want you to talk to me.

           You've been so quiet recently.

           It's when you go quiet . . .

           Don't want you to . . . I'm not going to see you in hospital again.

RUTH (con.): If you don't tell me that you're OK then I'm going to think.

Aren't I?

JANE: What do you want me to do? You want me to tell you I'm fine when I'm not?

RUTH: What do you want me to do? Crack open champagne every time you don't come home? Some mothers would. Believe me.

*There is an uneasy silence. **Jane** studies the floor, giving nothing away. Her mum looks back to the book.*

RUTH: Detective stories! I always know 'who dunnit' by page ten.

JANE: Yeah.

RUTH: I haven't noticed much good triumphing over evil round here, have you? (*She tries again*) Come down, there's pizza.

JANE: I'm going out.

RUTH: Jane, I don't think . . . you weren't home last night. You didn't call me. What am I supposed to do with you?

JANE: Nothing . . . I'm fine.

RUTH: I do need to talk to you. It's important. No, not about you! It's me and Rob. The house is nearly finished and . . .

JANE: I want to see Sam.

RUTH: Oh, love. (*She moves towards her*)

JANE:	What?
RUTH:	I would have taken you.
JANE:	No. There wasn't time.

Ruth moves towards *Jane* again; this time *Jane* moves away.

RUTH:	You'll find time.
JANE:	What do you mean?
RUTH:	To say goodbye.
JANE:	Whatever.
RUTH:	I've been thinking about him all morning.
JANE:	I don't think it was an accident, Mum.
RUTH:	What do you think?
JANE:	I think . . . no. It's OK, never mind.

She pulls on her jacket.

JANE:	Just being stupid. As usual. You wouldn't understand.
RUTH:	Where are you going now?
JANE:	For a walk.
RUTH:	Stay in, you don't look well.
JANE:	I'm fine, Mum.

Jane *exits.*

RUTH: I wonder where his mum is.

SCENE 2

Stephen, a 48 year old man and Adam, a 21 year old are outside in Stephen's garden. They're leaning up against the wall.

ADAM:　　　　Come on.

STEPHEN:　　I feel stupid.

ADAM:　　　　Come on. Be mean.

They kiss.

STEPHEN:　　(*Trying to be mean*) I want you.

They kiss harder.

ADAM:　　　　Good. Now. Come on. You know.

　　　　　　　　Rough.

STEPHEN:　　I want your arse.

Adam grabs Stephen and gets him to hold him against the wall.

ADAM:　　　　Yes?

STEPHEN:　　Your arse-hole.

ADAM:　　　　Errr!

　　　　　　　　OK. I'm like a rent-boy.

　　　　　　　　How much are you going to give me?

STEPHEN: (*Laughing*) Five bob.

ADAM: What? What's so funny?

STEPHEN: You're my little tart, aren't you? My little prick-tease.

ADAM: (*Mock innocence*) No. I'm just lost. I've got no money. I'll do whatever you want.

STEPHEN: You're a very naughty boy.

Stephen smacks *Adam's* bottom.

ADAM: Oh, that hurts.

STEPHEN: Are you OK?

ADAM: Of course I'm fucking OK. Don't stop!

STEPHEN: Oh. Sorry. Go on. Who are we again?

ADAM: We've just met, in a grotty little bar, never seen each other before, we're fucking before we've even spoken, I don't know your name, you don't know mine.

Go on. That's it. Fierce, be fierce, oh yes, bite me, go on bite me . . . really bite me.

Stephen bites him.

ADAM: Hurt me hard, tiger.

STEPHEN: They grunt, against the wall, where ants slip in and out.

ADAM: Hurt me, tiger.

STEPHEN: Yes.

ADAM: Hurt me!

STEPHEN: Hurt, but not harm.

Stephen bites him again.

ADAM: Oh yes. You're doing it. Get inside me!

STEPHEN: I am a tiger. A tiger, a fucking tiger fucking in the night. Magnificent. Power. I rule.

ADAM: Go on. Now.

STEPHEN: You're a cunt. A fucking prick-teasing cunt.

ADAM: Yes.

STEPHEN: Bitch, whore, cunt.

ADAM: Oh yes.

STEPHEN: You're a slice, a bitch, a whore, cunt, slag, tart, dog, a bit of skirt, she's a fag-bending shirt-lifting shit-stabbing queen, she's a bent fuck, fuck, fuck, fuck.

ADAM: Phew.

Adam turns round.

ADAM: You old dog.

Stephen slaps him hard.

ADAM: (*Shocked*) Ow!

STEPHEN: Too much?

ADAM: No. It's fine.

There's a straightening of clothes.

STEPHEN: Have you ever done that, for real?

ADAM: What do you mean?

STEPHEN: Rent.

ADAM: No.

             You?

STEPHEN: No.

ADAM: Money just doesn't mean anything when you really need
             it.

STEPHEN: Sorry?

ADAM: Nothing.

             You know it's all a bit old hat, all that.

STEPHEN: All what?

ADAM: Bitch, whore, queen business. I don't like being called 'she'
             either.

STEPHEN: Sorry. It's just what came out.

ADAM: S'all right, I thought you were wicked actually. I like the
             tiger. My father would love to say that; 'I fought a tiger with

ADAM (con.):	my bare hands in Africa.' Fucking twat. There aren't any tigers in Africa. Are there? As if my father could fight and kill something as pure as a fucking tiger, fucking twat.
STEPHEN:	I've got something for you.
ADAM:	Keys?
STEPHEN:	For here. You can come and go as you please. That is, when I'm away, conferences, you know, you can still come here. If you want to.
ADAM:	All right. Cheers.
STEPHEN:	God, you take me for granted.
ADAM:	I'm very grateful. (*Ruefully, rubbing his cheek*) Really.
STEPHEN:	I didn't mean to hurt you.
ADAM:	It's fine.

*They go inside. **Stephen** opens a bottle of beer and pours himself a whisky.*

STEPHEN:	I should have gone.
ADAM:	Why?
STEPHEN:	Respect.
ADAM:	Don't the dead bury themselves?
STEPHEN:	Yes.
	So when do your parents visit?

ADAM: End of term.

STEPHEN: Oh God!

ADAM: Don't worry.

             They would have preferred you to be a don.

STEPHEN: Unbelievable.

ADAM: They were so disappointed when I told them I was going to study in Swansea.

STEPHEN: They really don't mind?

ADAM: We're not going to talk about it over the Chablis!

STEPHEN: Oh. Right.

             They know how old I am?

ADAM: Yes.

             You'll like them.

             . . .

             As long as I'm successful what does it matter what I do with whom? Dollar is the only thing that really matters. And this hobby, it's so very English it's practically a tourist attraction. We'd be more odd to not carry on such a long and proud tradition.

STEPHEN: And you, are you proud of them?

ADAM: (*He considers for a moment*) I'm glad of them.

STEPHEN: I don't think the rough stuff is really me, you know.

ADAM: You're a natural.

STEPHEN: Shouldn't there be some rules? A safety net?

ADAM: Do tigers have rules?

STEPHEN: I suppose not.

ADAM: What would Blake say?

STEPHEN: Sooner murder an infant in its cradle than nurse unacted desires.

ADAM: See. (*Big kiss*)

STEPHEN: But whose, darling?

Whose desire?

SCENE 3

*Jane is talking to her stepdad, **Rob**, a 45 year old man. They are outside. He is gardening.*

JANE: You know what it feels like. It feels like this artist I heard of once. I don't know when exactly, or what his name was, but he was an artist before everything kicked off in Germany. And he used to paint enormous paintings, I can't remember who it was, saw it on the telly, I think, but the point was that before Hitler came along he was painting these enormous paintings, and they were probably really colourful, like messy and not of anything in particular but more like how you feel . . . and then Hitler comes and says 'Ooo that don't look like nothing' . . . and I don't know if he were a Jew but there he was and he didn't leave, at least I don't think he left, but the point was that even if he did leave what he had to do was make tiny little miniature drawings of the paintings he would've painted if he could. Maybe he was Russian, maybe he was scared of Stalin . . .

ROB: I'm glad you came down today.

JANE: Yeah . . . so maybe he was just poor and nobody would buy his big paintings but he carried on making them anyway, but just so small that he could fit them into his pocket, like postcards. And, you see, that's how I feel, I feel like I've got all these cool, beautiful postcards in my pocket but no one sees them, and I'm painting them and painting them but what good is it if nobody sees them? And then I get really frustrated because there isn't enough space, I try to squash it all into these edges, or I try and make them the size they're supposed to be and just think that one day I'll lay them out in a field and then I'll be able to see all of it, but the problem is while I'm

JANE (con.):	working on one I've forgotten what the others look like, and . . .
ROB:	I wanted to talk to you.
JANE:	Yeah, and maybe they don't match up, or I've missed out something important and they're probably all fucked any-way because . . .
ROB:	Don't.
JANE:	. . . but you don't understand what I'm saying. I'm keeping these little cards, but I'm not really keeping cards, I mean, that's like a metaphor for how I feel about my life, like no one gets why I hurt myself, but I could be doing plenty of other things that are completely acceptable like working too hard, or eating too much, or too little, or drinking, or smoking.
ROB:	You do smoke.
JANE:	Does Mum know?
ROB:	I haven't told her.
JANE:	I'm an artist. I mean, I can use it how I want to. See, I use my body just like an artist. It is my body, isn't it? 'Just be yourself.' Just not wacko Jacko. Did you ever feel like you weren't in your body?
ROB:	When I met your mum.
JANE:	(*Mock disgust*) Ooh!

ROB: And . . . I ran away from home once, didn't get far, but I remember looking through the fence at the end of the road, looking over the dump, hearing my heart thumping and then a train went past.

It's my first memory I think. I was five.

*He finds himself amusing, **Jane** is serious.*

JANE: Exactly. When I cut, I feel myself well up. I feel all the pain and beauty well up and then I can see it released. It's like, there in my throat like a dish I've wanted to eat for such a long time, and it tastes . . . ripe.

ROB: But it hurts.

JANE: It works.

ROB: For who?

***Jane** is momentarily startled. Pause. Thinks.*

JANE: Nurse in casualty. Do you know what she had the front to say to me? 'Stop wasting my time.'

Almost as bad as 'pull yourself together'.

ROB: They're under a lot of pressure.

JANE: Evil witch. She left me 'til last on purpose. What about the workaholics with heart attacks who never do any exercise, the smoking-related diseases, the stupid things people do when they're pissed. They'll put anyone in front of someone like me.

ROB: Jane.

JANE:	If they deserve help, why don't I? I wouldn't do it would I, if I didn't have to?

Long pause.

ROB:	Sam.
JANE:	What?
ROB:	You must miss him.
JANE:	No.
ROB:	Oh, come on!
JANE:	It seems like he's still here.
ROB:	He was too young . . . to be so alone.
JANE:	Life is shit.
ROB:	Yes . . . sometimes it is.
JANE:	I should go.
ROB:	I suppose I've done enough for today. Jane. What you're doing. I've seen it a lot. I've had friends, good friends when I was in the army, there was a lot of it and . . .
JANE:	Do you cut?
ROB:	No, but what I'm trying to say is . . .
JANE:	Have you ever cut?

ROB: No, but . . .

JANE: Then you don't know.

ROB: Look, I know I can't make you stop, but . . . oh, Christ.

JANE: (*To herself*) I *should* go.

ROB: Listen to me.

JANE: I need to see the sea. Is that stupid?

ROB: No. But . . .

JANE: There's something I've got to find out.

ROB: What?

JANE: Can I have some money?

ROB: No.

JANE: Come on.

ROB: No. Ruth wants to . . .

JANE: Don't worry about Mum. I'll go with Bethan. Won't be on my own. Want to breathe fresh air. Want an empty space. Change of scene. You know. I know you understand me. It'll make me happy.

ROB: Jane.

JANE: What's the point? What's the point if you don't trust me?

ROB: It's got nothing to do with trust.

JANE: Yes it has . . . I know you don't trust me.

          Why should you?

ROB: I do.

          Look, if I give you some money, you promise (*he gives her the money in his pocket*) you'll be back tonight?

JANE: Sure.

ROB: Jane.

JANE: Yes?

ROB: . . .

          Nothing.

          Good luck.

*He leaves and **Jane** takes the knife out of her pocket.*

SCENE 4

Adam and Stephen are in Stephen's living room, drinking.

STEPHEN: Have you thought any more about what you'll do when you finish?

ADAM: London first.

STEPHEN: First?

ADAM: Always liked the sound of New York.

STEPHEN: Plenty of trouble to get into there.

ADAM: That's what I thought.

STEPHEN: I'll miss you.

ADAM: Assuming I pass. Not for ages yet.

STEPHEN: You will. You're a very bright young man.

ADAM: Not to mention cute.

STEPHEN: Not to mention.

ADAM: You've got it sorted.

STEPHEN: Sorted?

ADAM: You've got young men on tap, haven't you? 'Excuse me, sir. I'm having difficulty with the essay titles.'

STEPHEN: Don't be ridiculous.

ADAM: Why do you think the rose is sick?

STEPHEN: You impertinent young scamp.

ADAM: Oh yeah?

*They wrestle to the ground, kiss. **Adam** breaks away.*

ADAM: So how many?

STEPHEN: You're the first.

ADAM: Come on.

STEPHEN: Really.

ADAM: Tell me. I won't tell.

STEPHEN: Honestly, darling. I've never had a relationship with a student before. It's not ethical.

ADAM: Ethical?

STEPHEN: I could lose my job.

ADAM: Hetty tutors are all at it. That slag Victoria's been banging Professor Paul Jones since freshers'.

STEPHEN: Maybe it would be all right. I would have to declare it, declare us, officially, if you were actually one of my students. In case anyone thought I was giving you preferential treatment.

ADAM: Would you?

STEPHEN: You're a very bright young man.

ADAM: And cute.

STEPHEN: Do you want to 'go public'?

ADAM: What's the point?

STEPHEN: Might make things easier for us.

ADAM: I'm not living with you or anything.

STEPHEN: No. But we love each other.

ADAM: What does that mean, for fuck's sake?

STEPHEN: I'm sorry. I just . . .

ADAM: Love is so for poofs.

Stephen pours another drink.

STEPHEN: So when you get to London, or New York, what are you going to do with all those brains and looks?

ADAM: Work my guts out in a job I'll hate until I'm so rich I can do whatever I like.

STEPHEN: It's not everything.

ADAM: I'm a coward.

STEPHEN: You're just young.

ADAM: If I had more guts I'd steal my millions. But I'll take whatever's on offer, that's not stealing that's just taking. I'm only saying what's true. Some men are so stupid, just

ADAM (con.): leaving it all out there to be taken. And then they're surprised when some bastard does take it.

I know I'm not cute really. No, it's OK, I know I'm not, I'm not even 'nice' . . . I don't even have 'a good personality.'

STEPHEN: You've got self-esteem issues.

ADAM: No. I just want sex. That's all. *Proud.* I'm . . . I'm a bit of a bastard.

STEPHEN: You're not a bastard any more than any of the other bastards.

ADAM: I don't want 'Love', Steve.

STEPHEN: Fine. I know.

Why don't we get really tight?

SCENE 5

*Jane and **Bethan** are driving at night. **Jane** is drinking.*

JANE: All right . . . favourite TV detective?

BETHAN: DCI Tennison.

JANE: Oh. I want her.

BETHAN: Bit obvious.

JANE: OK. You can have Helen Mirren if I can have J-Lo in *Out of Sight*.

BETHAN: That's a film!

JANE: OK, screen detective . . . Oooo no, I know. I want Jack Nicholson. *Chinatown*.

BETHAN: Faye Dunaway is way cool.

JANE: 'She's my daughter.'

**BETHAN/
JANE:**   'And my sister.'

                 (*Delighted disgust*) Ooooew!

Pause.

BETHAN: It's weird out here.

JANE: Abandoned.

BETHAN:	Those lights must be tankers. They're so slow. Do you think they're actually moving?
	Wouldn't like to be out here alone.
JANE:	Abandoned.
BETHAN:	Where are we going?
JANE:	To a B&B.
BETHAN:	Did you book one?
JANE:	We'll find one when we get there.
BETHAN:	Oh great, so we're sleeping in the car. Brilliant!
JANE:	We'll say we're sisters. You can be my sister.
BETHAN:	We don't particularly look like sisters.
JANE:	Oh, you could be a half-sister . . . they're not going to think twice.
BETHAN:	Jane, it's late, where are we going to find this B&B?
JANE:	Stop moaning. You didn't have to come, you know.
BETHAN:	How well did we really know him?
JANE:	He was my best friend.
BETHAN:	What about me?
JANE:	You're my girlfriend, it's different. I love you.

BETHAN: You're my best friend and I love you.

JANE: Sam needs me.

BETHAN: Yeah, well, Sam needed everyone. He needed everything. You don't even know where he really came from or why he was in Cardiff. You didn't even know where he was living from week to week. I saw him selling the *Big Issue* a month ago.

JANE: Well, that's good, isn't it?

BETHAN: Suppose, bet he only did it for a day though, 'til he found some new bloke to sponge off.

JANE: So harsh! You're always so harsh about Sam. He's dead. Killed. Can't you just have some pity for him?

BETHAN: And is that what you feel? Do you just feel sorry for him? Not much fucking friendship there then. I'm lucky you don't feel like I'm your best friend if that's how you feel about them. I wouldn't want your fucking pity.

SCENE 6

Ruth and *Rob* are in their kitchen. *Rob* is looking out the window, switching the light on and off outside and eating a chocolate bar. *Ruth* is cleaning the walls.

ROB: Those bloody foxes are out there again.

                      I swear they're bloody laughing at me, bloody bastards; they don't even eat them, they just dig them up. And then shit in my rose beds. Bastards.

RUTH: Yes dear.

ROB: Will you stop?

RUTH: It's nearly done.

ROB: You haven't answered my question.

RUTH: That's because I don't know, OK?

She stops and rinses out her cloth.

RUTH: You could help.

Rob picks up a cloth and starts to wipe the walls as well.

RUTH: Anyway, it's good for the earth, isn't it?

ROB: What?

RUTH: Manure.

ROB: I had a bit of a chat with Jane this afternoon.

Ruth stops.

ROB: Strange how sometimes she's so grown up and then so
          . . . young.

RUTH: What did she say?

ROB: She covered a few topics – history, art, modern life. But the
          special intelligence was that she took herself to casualty
          last night.

RUTH: I knew it. Oh God.

ROB: Now keep calm.

RUTH: I knew something was going on. It can't all just start again.
          Not now. Why? Why does she do it? (*Starts cleaning
          again*)

ROB: I don't think she knows.

RUTH: How can we stop her?

ROB: Don't know whether we can.

RUTH: I can't just sit back and let her . . .

          We were lucky.

          If it hadn't 've been for Bethan.

ROB: And Sam.

          I don't think she knows, you know, how bad it was last
          time.

RUTH (con.):   Maybe she doesn't think that anyone understands how she feels, but we all feel like that sometimes.

You have to just get on with things, don't you? I mean, what's the point in it?

ROB: When I was the same age as Jane I was learning how to kill people.

Everything was about pain. Pain reminded you you were still alive. That you were still feeling. Pain gave you hope.

It sets off survival responses. It's a drug in a way.

RUTH: Sometimes I think if she was taking drugs I could understand . . . I could understand wanting pleasure.

Is it because she's a lesbian? Bethan doesn't do it and she's much butcher than Jane . . . and Jane was never bullied like Bethan was.

ROB: What matters is that she stops.

RUTH: She won't talk to me any more.

ROB: We'll keep trying to find someone she can talk to . . . professionally.

RUTH: She talks to you.

ROB: Taunts me more like, then wraps me round her little finger.

RUTH: Is it my fault?

ROB: No. Don't think that.

RUTH:	I'm a useless mother. Can't protect her.
ROB:	You can't save people from themselves.
RUTH:	Don't tell me that.
ROB:	(*Puts his arms around her*) You do protect her. It'll be all right. She's a survivor deep down.
RUTH:	Where is she? She didn't come home with you?
ROB:	No, she should be back soon though.
RUTH:	Back? Back from where?
ROB:	Oh. She's gone on a trip to the seaside with Bethan.
RUTH:	'A trip to the seaside?'
ROB:	She was upset about Sam.
RUTH:	All the more reason for her not to be gallivanting off to the sea with her bucket and bloody spade.
ROB:	She wanted to go and 'clear her head' she said. Bethan is going with her.
RUTH:	Clear her head?
	And how is she paying for this little trip?
ROB:	Well . . .
RUTH:	What?

ROB:	I gave her some money, but she's coming back tonight. She promised.
RUTH:	Where is she? Which 'seaside'? How is she getting there?
	What if she doesn't come back?
	How can you be so irresponsible?
	After what she told you!
ROB:	What else could I do?
RUTH:	Brought her bloody home!
ROB:	We can't lock her up. We might not like it . . . but we can't stop her. She's an adult . . . practically.
RUTH:	Easy for you to say, she's not your daughter.
ROB:	Oh.
RUTH:	I mean . . .
ROB:	No, I know what you mean.
RUTH:	No you don't. I didn't mean that.
ROB:	You know, married or not, she is . . . I am her parent, if not her father. If you don't like that . . .
RUTH:	I do like that. You know I do.
	But I'm terrified.
	I'm terrified of what she might do.

RUTH (con.): I'm her mother.

How could you let her go?

ROB: She's going to be all right. I promise.

RUTH: But you can't.

SCENE 7

*The car is parked. **Bethan** is holding **Jane**. They have curled up in the car under their coats. **Sam** is sitting in the car.*

SAM:
You're giving up on me. I staggered all along this bank, in the dark. I was left to die. You don't care about me. All you care about is yourself.

BETHAN:
Remind me, why are we out here in the freezing cold? (*Under her breath*) Oh, silly me, I forgot. Sam.

JANE:
I'm not cold.

BETHAN:
That'll be the vodka.

SAM:
Selfish cow.

JANE:
I knew a boy who had a beautiful voice. When he spoke, people's knees trembled. His parents were clever and sent him to work quickly. He never really understood what his job was. But then he never thought about it, so he didn't worry very much about it.

SAM:
Go on, make up nice little fairy stories for your girlfriend. She never spoke to me. She always looked right through me. She don't care about me. She probably don't care about you.

JANE:
One day an especially rich lady bought him. He had to get up at the same time she did and read the paper to her over her breakfast. She would take him with her on trips to friends' houses and to the shops. Often he would be asked to sing for her friends. Then they would give him presents, little kisses and secret notes to call them when

JANE (con.):   their husbands weren't home and talk to them over the phone.

SAM: I know exactly what I am.

JANE: The arrangement was very proper. He slept in the far end of the house to where his mistress slept. He had been brought up to always be dressed very smartly. He would never dream of being seen without a shirt on, for example. He had never seen anyone's body other than his own. This was for the very good reason that his parents loved him and they didn't want their son to know that not everyone's torso is covered with feathers. His plumage was soft and downy brown. They felt it was the unfortunate side-effect of being gifted with such a beautiful voice.

SAM: (*Angry*) I'm bored.

JANE: One night his mistress was ill. She brayed terrible moans along the lonely corridors. He was so scared that he ran to her room, yet even in his fear and distress he pulled a shirt on to protect his modesty. As he burst into his mistress's room he saw her in the pool of moonlight in a state of high fever. Her nightdress had fallen off. He saw her breasts, the most beautiful things he had ever seen, and a glistening stomach, as smooth as glass. Not a wrinkle or hair spoiled the pure line, the smooth landscape of her body, the moisture from her fever ran in fine, unfettered lines to the bed.

He left immediately, called for the doctor and waited outside her room until she recovered. But while he waited he thought about her body, how beautiful it was, how she had ruffled his feathers. He realised that her beauty would stop him sleeping; his heart beat, his stomach fluttered, his mind soared. He had fallen in love, he felt his soft feathers so disturbed in the commotion and felt disgust. He looked

48

JANE (con.): at his body, and wondered at his blindness. How had he never seen the smoothness of skin before, never wondered at the difference so plain now between himself and those around him? He didn't know where to go, but he had to leave; where could he hide himself? Even from himself?

BETHAN: You're very beautiful.

*Leans over to kiss **Jane** but **Sam** stops **Jane**.*

SAM: Find my killer.

***Jane** puts on music. Time passes. **Jane** and **Bethan** wake up to the dawn. **Sam** stays asleep.*

BETHAN: How's your head?

JANE: Fine. Right. Where should we start? He could be any of those people out there.

BETHAN: Who?

JANE: The killer.

BETHAN: The what?

JANE: I told you that Sam came to me.

BETHAN: Was I there when you told me?

JANE: He came and told me that he'd been murdered and that I had to find out who did it.

BETHAN: And then what?

JANE: Bring him or her to justice.

BETHAN:	You don't really believe that you're – what? Haunted? Psychic? Sam is dead.
JANE:	Yeah. I know.
BETHAN:	There are no such things as ghosts.
JANE:	He wants me to find his killer.
BETHAN:	Jane, he's dead. He couldn't
JANE:	Will you stop saying that? I know.
BETHAN:	OK. He was really a great guy, OK, and your best friend and you loved him and it's not fair because he isn't here any more and he should be. I know he didn't have it easy. But you can't bring him back with stories or ghosts. It won't help. Not really.
JANE:	He's here.
BETHAN:	Where? I'm here but I'm more like a ghost to you than Sam is. This is reality. Me. Will you just snap out of it?!
JANE:	Pull myself together?
BETHAN:	When Nana died I was angry with everything, everyone. If you were angry, even with me, I'd understand.
JANE:	I am angry with you. Sam needs me. And you're just jealous.
BETHAN:	(*Tries to hold her hand*) Jane, I love you.
JANE:	Don't do that.
BETHAN:	What? I'm just trying.

JANE:	Not here. I don't feel safe.
BETHAN:	There's no one here.
JANE:	You never know who's going to walk past.
BETHAN:	Stop being so paranoid.
JANE:	Don't call me paranoid.

Bethan still holds Jane's hand, but less lovingly.

BETHAN:	Sam wasn't an easy person to be around.
SAM:	(*Waking up*) What's she saying about me?
JANE:	Don't you dare. Don't you dare talk about Sam. You . . . you don't even believe in him.
BETHAN:	He never helped you. He never tried to help you stop hurting yourself.
SAM:	That's not true.
BETHAN:	You had nothing in common.
SAM:	Now that's just not true.
BETHAN:	You saw what he was like that time in King's. He was looking for trouble. I've never been so glad to see someone . . . just stop . . . when he collapsed, you know . . .
SAM:	Yeah . . . I did overdo it a bit that night . . . I'll give her that.
JANE:	You don't know the first thing about Sam.

BETHAN:	And what do you know? (*She lets go of Jane's hand*) You were just delighted that you had finally found someone even more pitiful than yourself.
JANE:	Are you quoting your dad? Or is this what you think?
BETHAN:	What's my dad got to do with anything?
JANE:	Just that you think the sun shines out of his arse.
BETHAN:	You know, I wouldn't be surprised if he was killed actually. He was looking for it.
SAM:	(*Angry*) Yeah, the tart deserved what he got.
JANE:	What?
BETHAN:	He was asking for trouble. Every day. Camping it up around town.
SAM:	'I am what I am.'
JANE:	If he was a girl would you say that?
SAM:	I was fucking fabulous.
BETHAN:	What?
JANE:	If you wore a short skirt and then got raped, would that be your fault?
BETHAN:	You've got to look after yourself. The world isn't going to change, you can't just shut your eyes and pretend it's safe. You've got to understand that.
JANE:	You don't know what he'd been through.

BETHAN: Do you? You're like two addicts together. So what's your excuse?

JANE: What about me?

BETHAN: How long's it going to be before you get washed up?

But then I guess you'll just grow out of it.

JANE: Yeah, maybe it's just a phase I'm going through.

Or maybe you're just a phase I'm going through.

BETHAN: You don't mean that. I'm only trying.

JANE: Fuck fuck fuck you.

Bethan gets out, walks off, then comes back.

BETHAN: I need some money to get home.

JANE: (*Getting out*) Here, why don't you take the car?

BETHAN: What am I going to say to your mum and Rob?

JANE: Whatever.

BETHAN: Don't you think I've had enough? Had enough of all your shit?

Listen to me.

JANE: Just fuck off, Bethan

BETHAN: Great. Just fucking brilliant. Fine.

Good luck!

SCENE 8

Jane and Sam are walking along the coastline.

SAM: It wasn't her.

Jane looks around to make sure she's alone, then sits down and unwraps her bandages.

JANE: No. She didn't like you but she wouldn't have killed you.

SAM: She's not a fuck-up like us.

JANE: She's the only thing that makes any sense.

She takes out the knife and opens up the wound on her right arm with it.

SAM: Just me and you now, treacle.

She watches the blood ooze from the wound then rewraps her arm.

JANE: Shhh.

SCENE 9

*Birds dance in the air. **Stephen**, carrying a paper wrap of chips, is being attacked by seagulls. **Jane** walks along the side of the estuary; **Sam** is docile, following a few steps behind.*

STEPHEN: Fuck off, you little shits!

JANE: They're after yer chips.

STEPHEN: Excuse me?

JANE: Your chips, that's what they want. They're like a steal of seagulls.

STEPHEN: Colony of seagulls actually.

JANE: Right.

STEPHEN: But such a dull collective noun for such bandits does seem churlish.

JANE: Could be steel, like metal, as well. They're real grey and hard close up.

STEPHEN: Little shits, when they're not stealing your meal they're depositing their last one on your head.

JANE: But the shapes they make.

STEPHEN: Free as a bird, so far away.

JANE: . . . have a . . . nice day.

Jane carries on past him.

STEPHEN: Yes. You too.

*Sam catches up with **Jane***.

SAM: It's him. It's him.

JANE: Really?

SAM: Yeah. Yeah. Think about it. Gay, old, posh, rich. Just my type, not the type to live near here, I was killed two miles from here remember . . . so what's he doing hanging around . . . eating chips?!

JANE: He is suspect.

SAM: Prime, I'd say.

Stephen throws his bag of chips away.

STEPHEN: (*To the birds*) Just bloody take them.

JANE: What are you doing?

STEPHEN: I wish I knew.

JANE: Someone was killed near here.

STEPHEN: What is it about this place?

JANE: What do you mean?

STEPHEN: Someone I knew committed suicide here, not far from here.

SAM: He's talking about me. I knew him.

JANE: Who was that?

56

STEPHEN:	Sam. Samuel. I think.
JANE:	Sam Clarke?
STEPHEN:	I didn't know what his surname was.
JANE:	Bit taller than me? Blond hair, blue eyes?
STEPHEN:	Yes . . . he was without permanent address, I believe.
SAM:	See? See?
STEPHEN:	You knew him?
JANE:	I might have.
STEPHEN:	I was speculating.
JANE:	What?
STEPHEN:	What a nice young lady would be doing wandering around on her own out here. It is rather gloomy.
SAM:	Ask him.
JANE:	What are you doing here?
STEPHEN:	I suppose I wanted to . . . pay my respects. Stupid thing is . . . this is as far as I can go. Didn't think I was squeamish.
	I didn't know him very well but I feel quite shaken. The funeral was on Saturday and I just couldn't face it and then I thought coming here would be a more appropriate way to honour his life.

STEPHEN (con.): Unforgivably sentimental. I know. You should 'drive your cart and your plough over the bones of the dead', but how?

JANE: What?

STEPHEN: It's one of the Devil's proverbs, so probably best take it with a pinch of salt.

JANE: The Devil?

STEPHEN: I'm Stephen.

JANE: Sorry?

STEPHEN: Stephen Jefferies. I teach at the University, English literature. William Blake mostly. I'm a William Blake obsessive.

Do you read?

JANE: Yeah, suppose.

STEPHEN: I told him, the road of excess leads to the palace of wisdom. He was rather slow. I hope he didn't take too much notice of me.

JANE: What do you mean 'slow'?

STEPHEN: What's your name?

JANE: You don't need to know who I am.

STEPHEN: No. No. I don't. Quite right.

JANE: What do you mean 'slow'?

STEPHEN: I suppose he had a certain native intelligence. Street wisdom as it were. But I don't think he'd darkened many school doors.

JANE: Do you think because he didn't go to school he deserved to die?

STEPHEN: No. Of course not.

JANE: He's really funny.

STEPHEN: So you *did* know him?

JANE: Better than you. Better than anyone.

STEPHEN: What about his family?

JANE: We were family.

STEPHEN: I used to have friends like that.

He offers her a cigarette.

JANE: (*Grunts*) Thanks.

STEPHEN: There is a blank sort of beauty about this place. An oblivion in those graduations from slate sea to china sky. It's all so monochrome and then a sliver of light seems like a miracle of colour. Like seeing angels. Wish I could see angels.

JANE: Don't believe in angels.

STEPHEN: No?

What's your favourite colour?

JANE: Purple . . . and green.

STEPHEN: Wimbledon colours and suffragette colours.

JANE: You what?

STEPHEN: Joke. The miracle of colour.

             You see, I like pink.

JANE: Pink carnations for pansies.

STEPHEN: Yes. (*He offers her an arm*) And lavender for appearances.
             My car's just up here. Do you want an ice?

SAM: Don't be scared. Remember you're doing it for me.

JANE: (*To Stephen*)   All right.

She doesn't take the arm but follows him off.

SCENE 10

Ruth is in the kitchen. Rob comes in.

RUTH: Well?

ROB: No. Bethan didn't come home either. That means they're still together. They'll be back soon. Try not to worry.

Rob takes a cigarette out of Ruth's packet, she takes one, he lights it.

RUTH: Get your own sodding fags.

Rob lights up.

RUTH: You never think, do you?

Rob blows the smoke in a long, thin line, puts out the cigarette and starts to pace.

RUTH: They're seventeen, for God's sake.

                    Don't worry! Ha. How can you just say they'll be back? They might not be. Look at what happened to Sam.

ROB: I was the same age when I left home. They're not defence-less. They've got the car, phones, money.

RUTH: Jane's not you . . . she's not like you . . . it's different.

ROB: I know, but what I'm trying to say . . .

RUTH: You were in barracks. You were protected. You didn't have to think for yourself. You just did what you were told.

ROB: You don't know what you're talking about.

RUTH: Oh my God. You did it on purpose, didn't you?

ROB: What?

RUTH: You! You think that this is some kind of test.

ROB: No. Jesus Christ. I'm going out of my bloody mind here.

I had no choice.

Will you just stop?

RUTH: Me? It's not me.

ROB: You're as bad as she is sometimes.

RUTH: You saying it's my fault?!

ROB: See . . . see . . . that . . . that's what I mean . . . defensive aggression, that's what that is.

RUTH: Oh my God. I'll show you aggressive aggression if you don't shut up.

She's got you wrapped around her little finger.

ROB: And you want to wrap her up in cotton wool.

RUTH: No, Rob, what I would like is for those lines on her arms, on her legs and stomach, do you know the ones I mean . . .? Not even the ones she made herself; no, it's the lines that the doctors made when they stitched her up that really bother me, the ones that make my little girl look like she's been patched together out of other people's limbs and

RUTH (con.):	skin, like she's Frankenstein's bloody bride . . . Oh, God . . . I can't bear it, I can't bear to think like this . . . I think these . . . I think these things about my own little girl.
ROB:	Come here.
RUTH:	No. Why did you let her go?
ROB:	She stole the car . . . you can't blame me for that!
RUTH:	You left the keys out.
ROB:	I thought she'd take the bus.
RUTH:	How much did you give her?
ROB:	I only gave her ten quid.
RUTH:	She's taken thirty out of my purse!
	She's never stolen from me before.
	Christ in heaven. Is this going to be it? Is it?
ROB:	Stop shouting.
RUTH:	God!

She finds a plate and drops it on the floor quite deliberately. She listens to the noise.

ROB:	Better?
RUTH:	(*She drops another, listening again*) Yes.
ROB:	You're making a mess.

RUTH: They're only plates.

ROB: Will you please just calm down, Ruth?

He starts to clear the pieces.

RUTH: Leave it.

ROB: Stop.

RUTH: What's the point? You can't control anything. You can't protect the people you love.

Smashes another.

ROB: Let's try to think rationally.

RUTH: The people you love smash you up. The more you love them the more they smash you.

Smashing continues.

RUTH: You feel like an idiot, like a failure, like a punch-bag, but you keep going back for more smashing.

ROB: Stop it, Ruth.

RUTH: So you can see where she gets it from.

ROB: Ruth.

RUTH: See! (*Smashes another one*) It *is* my fault.

ROB: No.

RUTH: I'm a bad mother. I'm selfish. I want to be happy. I want you.

RUTH (con.):   I want my job. I want my friends and my beautiful home.

Is it so bad to be happy? I've had to work so hard for every single scrap of happiness.

I've worked hard to be happy. I rebuilt my whole life and now I'm bloody happy.

More plates.

ROB: Just bloody stop it.

RUTH: Bloody make me.

She smashes another plate. **Rob** *grabs hold of her.*

RUTH: Go on then.

ROB: I'm not going to hit you. I could. I could very easily. But I am not going to hit you.

I could put my hand over your mouth. I could stop you shouting at me. I would really like to stop this . . . this . . . stress.

I want to hurt . . . to . . . punish the person who made you and Jane this unhappy.

But I can't, can I?

. . .

Can I?

RUTH: No.

Rob lets go. He is shaking with nervous anxiety.

ROB: It's never going to be like that between us. It can't be. I won't be bullied . . . bullied like this . . . Ruth . . . do you understand? . . . Do you understand?

RUTH: Yes.

SCENE 11

Jane and Stephen are both eating ice-creams. They are sitting on a bench overlooking the sea. Sam is sitting between them.

STEPHEN: We're lucky it was open. Beautiful here, in ice-cream season. Had a boyfriend once who liked it here. It is 'outstandingly beautiful'. Officially. How do you judge a thing like that do you think? The Gower is a high first but Shropshire only a good 2.1? Does it last forever? I used to be beautiful, be loved. But now my grades have slipped.

JANE: Whatever.

STEPHEN: Quite right. So what do you want to know?

JANE: Er . . .

SAM: Scaredy cat, scaredy cat, don't know what you're looking at.

STEPHEN: Is it nice?

JANE: What?

STEPHEN: Your ice.

SAM: I remember eating ice-cream. My favourite was Neapolitan, that's not really a flavour, that's three flavours for the price of one.

Long pause.

STEPHEN: Look. I have a date. I was planning to sit here in peace until my beau arrives. Can't you be civil and just chat to

67

STEPHEN (con.): an old man? I only have a certain amount of peace in my life and you're spoiling it.

JANE: Right.

Sam is looking at the ice-cream.

SAM: The home did fish and chips with Neapolitan ice-cream for afters every Friday.

Jane scratches at her bandages.

STEPHEN: Shhh.

                 . . .

                 All right. Out with it. What bee is buzzing around your bonnet?

SAM: Mum's fish and chips was much better because she bought it from a proper fish and chip shop . . . none of this freezer shit.

                 Find out why I'm dead.

JANE: I've received some information.

STEPHEN: What sort of information?

JANE: I can't tell you that at the moment, but all you need to know is that I know he was killed.

STEPHEN: Oh yes, you said. Not suicide but murder most foul.

SAM: What was he doing on the night I was killed? And how did I get out there? Ask him that.

JANE: How did Sam get out there? He never left Cardiff, especially in the winter.

STEPHEN: He was on the game.

JANE: So?

STEPHEN: It wasn't exactly unusual for him to get into strange men's cars.

SAM: Perhaps I got into his car one night.

JANE: You know a lot about it.

STEPHEN: He was a well-known face.

SAM: Perhaps I did him, then stole his gold bracelet that belonged to his dead mother and in a fit of rage he murdered me for it.

JANE: Did you and him . . ?

STEPHEN: Good God, no.

I felt . . . parental.

Not that anyone would believe me. Perhaps he reminded me of myself when I was beautiful and innocent. It amazed me that he could live so hard but still be so innocent.

JANE: What were you doing on the twentieth of February?

STEPHEN: Look. The last time I saw him he was drunk. I was really concerned about him. We talked about protection. You know, from diseases. I asked him if he was 'safe' and he said 'I've got my seat-belt on.'

Jane and Sam look at each other and laugh.

STEPHEN: He wasn't being funny.

He wasn't joking.

Chaotic . . . that's what he was.

I was trying to help him. He was so drunk he could hardly talk. He got in my car. I thought I'd take him home, let him sleep it off, better than being on the streets. He suddenly came to, opened the door and threw himself out on to the road. I was about to pull away from the lights. There were cars all around me. I looked back and he was on his feet, making his way back to the bars, in that direction anyway.

JANE: He got run over once. He broke his leg.

SAM: I have broken both ankles, my hip, my right knee, four ribs and some bones in this hand.

STEPHEN: What were you doing on the twentieth?

It's only fair, isn't it?

JANE: (*Quiet*) I wasn't feeling very well.

SAM: Poor little Janey Waney.

JANE: I went to hospital.

SAM: Two weeks in intensive care, me . . . morphine drip . . . the works . . . and I escaped as soon as I could walk.

STEPHEN: How did you meet him?

JANE:	First time I went to King's.
STEPHEN:	Can be intimidating.
SAM:	Home from home.
JANE:	Like starting at a new school. Don't know anyone, not sure if you're wearing the right clothes, there's even a door monitor.
STEPHEN:	Do I fit in?
JANE:	You go in and it's packed.
	Stinks of sweat, deodorant and amyl. Even in gay bars men look at girls, perhaps not like they'd looked at Sam . . . but still. There was a small group of women a lot older than me in the far corner, they were completely wrapped up in themselves, drinking and laughing, I saw one of them break off, she seemed less part of the group than the others and I followed her into the loos. We talked a bit. Massive queue; waited for ages; you know what those loos used to be like.
STEPHEN:	Did this girl and you . . .?
SAM:	'Bash the beaver'?
JANE:	No!
	I was fourteen. I knew I was gay. I knew it was a gay bar. I thought all I had to do was put the two together. All I needed to do was get in there and that would be it, I'd be 'out'.
STEPHEN:	Eternal irony of the closet.

JANE:	Met Sam outside.
SAM:	Been thrown out for sucking some bloke's cock in the bogs.
JANE:	He'd been caught . . . in the toilets.
STEPHEN:	Really.
JANE:	So unfair. The other bloke stayed inside because he was old enough to drink. I'd thrown myself out. No one to talk to. We sat on the castle wall all night and drank cider. He's a month younger than me.
STEPHEN:	So you became Best Friends?
SAM:	Best Friends?
JANE:	He's mine.
STEPHEN:	Just because he died a long way from Cardiff doesn't mean he was killed. Wasn't he from London originally?
JANE:	Yes. Well, I'm not sure.
SAM:	Did you ask?
STEPHEN:	It seems to me there's not much you are sure of. I know you gals love those detective stories but . . .
JANE:	What?
STEPHEN:	It's just like the boys with *Star Wars* and *Dr Who* isn't it? You're no more a detective than I'm a spaceman.
JANE:	I know he shouldn't be dead. I know that I'm the only one

JANE (con.): who gives a shit about what happened to him and that he trusts me.

STEPHEN: He trusted you.

SAM: I don't know why you're feeling sorry for yourself.

JANE: I'm not feeling sorry for myself.

STEPHEN: You mean he trusted you?

SAM: I did trust you . . . but now look at you. You're going to bits.

STEPHEN: What do you mean?

SAM: I can't trust you. You're going to let him get away with it. I'm dead!

JANE: You do trust me.

STEPHEN: Sorry?

JANE: I didn't mean . . . nothing! All right?

She is biting back tears.

JANE: I don't mean anything.

STEPHEN: Is there something you want to tell me?

JANE: No.

SAM: Tell him about me.

JANE: No. He won't understand

STEPHEN:	Who won't understand?
JANE:	You, you won't understand
STEPHEN:	(*Getting angry*) Did he tell you he was going to kill himself?
JANE:	No!
STEPHEN:	What are you hiding?
JANE:	Nothing.
STEPHEN:	All right. Sorry. I didn't mean to shout.
JANE:	He still trusts me.
STEPHEN:	I'm sorry?
JANE:	I'm losing it.
STEPHEN:	Deep breaths.
JANE:	I wish I were dead.
STEPHEN:	It's all right. Just take it slowly.
JANE:	Sam.
STEPHEN:	Yes.
JANE:	He's with me, here.
	I mean it's like he is really here. Like not even his ghost, but him. Like he's not dead at all.
STEPHEN:	I see.

JANE: He can still wind me up and make me do what he wants.

STEPHEN: What does he want?

JANE: He says he was killed. That I have to go to where he was killed; that he is bored being dead; that it's shit; that he misses me. I can't let him down. OK? I just can't let him down.

STEPHEN: OK. OK. It's all a bit much.

He passes her a handkerchief.

JANE: Ta.

STEPHEN: Mop up.

So you think that Sam is visiting you from the other side?

JANE: You taking the piss?

STEPHEN: Not at all.

I wish people would visit me more often.

JANE: You are taking the piss.

STEPHEN: I'm not, honestly. But it's not very nice for you, is it?

JANE: Nice?

STEPHEN: Is he here, now?

JANE: Yes.

STEPHEN: (*Whispering*) I don't think you should trust him. He's dead. He's changed. He can never be the person he was.

SAM: You can't trust him.

JANE: I can't trust anyone.

Do you think I'm mad?

STEPHEN: I don't know.

JANE: I've got to find out what happened.

STEPHEN: You're grieving. You don't know what you're doing. I think you should go home.

SAM: No! You can't go home.

JANE: You ever hurt someone and not even know why you did it?

STEPHEN: Oh. Much better than that.

JANE: Mum, Bethan, Rob, Sam . . .

STEPHEN: We all hurt people, you can't help it, especially if you love them.

JANE: Can't you?

STEPHEN: Who wants a painless life anyway?

JANE: Don't you?

STEPHEN: Sometimes being hurt reminds you that you care.

JANE: Eh?

STEPHEN: But harm . . . that's something else. The question is which is which?

STEPHEN (con.): I would never try to harm anyone.

JANE: I have to find out who killed him.

STEPHEN: I'm a clod. Do you know what that means?

JANE: Clumsy?

STEPHEN: Not in this case. I'm like a soft piece of clay. You can push me around. I believe in Love, with a capital 'L'. I believe in feelings and caring about people. It makes you open, vulnerable. Soft. If you love someone they can hurt you so much.

JANE: Like if they leave you?

STEPHEN: Exactly. My . . . my . . . (*tries to find the right word*) my lover doesn't believe in Love. He's frightened of getting hurt so he behaves like a smooth, hard little pebble, impervious and self-contained.

JANE: He does your head in?

STEPHEN: Yes.

You would think that someone who is as soft as clay like me couldn't hurt anyone . . . quite the contrary. I went behind his back. Followed him. Watched him meet up with his bit of rough.

And made sure it ended.

JANE: Bit of rough?

STEPHEN: If I don't tell you then I'll have you on my conscience as well as Sam and . . .

JANE:	Tell me what?
STEPHEN:	I threatened Sam.
JANE:	What?
STEPHEN:	To tell the authorities where he was living, get him sent back home or put back into care or wherever it was he was supposed to be. I just wanted him to stop seeing Adam.
	I wanted Adam. I wasn't thinking about Sam. He was terrified of being found, it wasn't hard to persuade him not to see Adam any more.
JANE:	You bastard.
STEPHEN:	It wasn't my fault he killed himself.
JANE:	He didn't kill himself.
SAM:	No!
STEPHEN:	Yes. I had no right to scare him.
JANE:	When was this?
STEPHEN:	A month ago.
JANE:	He never seemed scared of anything. Even now. He's not scared. Just angry.
SAM:	That's right. I'm not scared of you.
STEPHEN:	I'll give you a lift to the station.

JANE:	Aren't you meeting your 'whatever' now?
STEPHEN:	He won't be here for a while.
JANE:	I should wait for him.
STEPHEN:	No.
JANE:	Yes. I think I should meet this Adam.
STEPHEN:	Don't say anything to him, please.
JANE:	Why should I do what you want?

*Sam sings an angry song. **Jane** watches him. When the song has finished she turns and shakes hands with **Adam**, who is looking very hungover.*

JANE:	Hallo.
ADAM:	Who are you?
JANE:	I knew Sam. Sam Clarke.
ADAM:	Sam Francisco?
SAM:	I never told you about Adam, did I?
JANE:	What?
ADAM:	What about him?
JANE:	Um, well. He meant a lot to me and I thought I'd go and pay my last respects to him. You know. Flowers or something, but I didn't get that far, had an argument with my girlfriend actually, and I met your boyfriend on the way and he made me realise I didn't know Sam at all, so we

JANE (con.):	thought since you knew Sam too that you might know what he was doing out there, all on his own, coz I just can't understand it, and I've just got this really weird feeling I could find out what happened, really. Can you help me, at all, do you think?
ADAM:	No.
SAM:	He's a git.
ADAM:	What do you want me to say? I can't.
	I hardly knew him. We went out for a few drinks, Stephen and I had a few drinks with him if he was out when we were. That's it. I know a hundred people who I only ever talk to half pissed. You couldn't know anyone less.
	Were you like a proper friend?
JANE:	Suppose.
ADAM:	I didn't think he had those. Sorry. Really.
STEPHEN:	Don't, Adam.
ADAM:	What? I mean it. Don't know what more I can say.
JANE:	When was the last time you saw him?
ADAM:	Ages ago.
SAM:	Be specific.
JANE:	Try and remember. Would mean a lot to me.
STEPHEN:	What harm can it do? It'll only take a few seconds.

ADAM: God my head is banging.

SAM: Stop fucking around.

JANE: Just answer the question.

ADAM: What are you like?!

          Six months ago. OK? It was at least six months ago.

JANE: Are you sure?

SAM: He's lying. He is so lying.

ADAM: Yeah. It was the seventeenth of August, Mam and I remember because it was my birthday. (*Indicates Stephen*) We went out for dinner and then to King's after, and he was there, like he always was. I don't even know if I said hallo.

JANE: Tell me how you met.

ADAM: Why?

JANE: I want to know what happened.

ADAM: He was a fickle jade.

JANE: How did you . . .?

ADAM: What fucking difference does it make now? He's dead and gone. What's the point of indulging yourself in how sad it all is? He's dead, you're not. I'm not. Cool.

JANE: You're a fucking bastard.

ADAM: Bitch, please!

SAM: They're in it together. (*Indicates Adam*) He spiked my drink, then suffocated me and then (*indicates Stephen*) he threw my body in the mud.

JANE: When did you last see him?

STEPHEN: I've got an idea.

                Why don't we buy some flowers and do the right thing by him? That's what you came to do, so let's do it.

SAM: Go on . . . go on . . . this is it.

JANE: OK.

ADAM: OK what?

JANE: OK let's go.

ADAM: Stephen?

STEPHEN: You said you were sorry. Or is there more to it?

ADAM: No. It's just a waste of time.

                Afternoon.

Sam sings again. They are all in **Stephen**'s car.

ADAM: What are we doing?

                This is a nightmare. (*He pulls out some bottles of beer*) Got an opener?

STEPHEN: Sorry.

ADAM:	Don't suppose you have?
JANE:	Can't you use your teeth?
ADAM:	I don't think so!
JANE:	If I can open one can I have one?
ADAM:	Sounds like a deal.

Jane pulls out her knife and prises off the tops of two beer bottles.

ADAM:	Cheers.
JANE:	Cheers.
STEPHEN:	He was a nice lad, basically.
SAM:	Like you'd know.
JANE:	(*Firmly*) Shhh.
ADAM:	Shhh yourself.
	(*To Stephen*) You didn't know him.
STEPHEN:	We both did.
ADAM:	He was just an acquaintance.
STEPHEN:	I gave him a lift once, had quite a chat.
ADAM:	Did you?
STEPHEN:	I did most of the talking actually, he was paralytic. I didn't think it was safe for him to be out.

ADAM: When was this?

STEPHEN: A month ago.

ADAM: Oh. Right. You never mentioned it.

STEPHEN: Didn't I?

It wasn't important. I had forgotten myself, but then Jane here was asking me all these questions about Sam and I remembered that I had offered to put him up for the night and he was going to come back. But then he had a change of heart.

JANE: What made him change his mind?

STEPHEN: When I told him where I lived.

Maybe he'd had a bad experience in the Mumbles. Mumblephobic perhaps?

JANE: So, Adam, what do you think happened to Sam?

ADAM: Don't know.

JANE: Do you think that he could have been murdered?

ADAM: What, and someone made it look like suicide? And didn't leave any marks or evidence of any kind? Yeah, I think that's really likely.

JANE: Don't you think it's strange that he was all the way out here?

ADAM: What difference does it make either way? Why do you want to know what his last breath was like? Satisfy some morbid curiosity? Get your emotional rocks off over the dead

ADAM (con.): homeless boy. He led a dangerous life. He took enormous risks.

JANE: But it's wrong.

ADAM: Wrong? I don't know what's right and wrong. I'd rather live sixteen interesting years than a hundred boring ones.

STEPHEN: Smooth and impervious aren't you, darling?

ADAM: He's a statistic now.

But he'll be young forever. The emperor Hadrian had a boy who killed himself, drowned himself on the banks of the Nile rather than lose his looks and the love of the great man.

JANE: You're not exactly an emperor.

SAM: The Queen of Sketty.

JANE: Jesus! (*She jumps out of her skin*) Shut up.

STEPHEN: You all right?

JANE: Sorry. Yes, I'm fine.

ADAM: Perhaps you shouldn't have that (*referring to the beer*).

JANE: I'm fine.

SAM: I was the one who dumped him, remember.

JANE: He dumped you, not the other way round.

ADAM: I'm sorry?

JANE:	He dumped you.
ADAM:	Did he talk about me?
JANE:	You're trying to say that he killed himself for you, like the Roman boy.
ADAM:	Did he tell you about me? What did he say?
SAM:	Little mummy's boy.
JANE:	He said you were a mummy's boy.
ADAM:	No, that doesn't sound like him.
STEPHEN:	How well did you know him?
ADAM:	I told you, we went out a few times.
STEPHEN:	Actually you didn't tell me.
SAM:	(*Sing-song voice*) They're gonna have a fight . . . they're gonna have a fight.
ADAM:	Didn't I?
STEPHEN:	You know you didn't.
ADAM:	Didn't think it was important.
STEPHEN:	Not important!
ADAM:	What's it got to do with you?
STEPHEN:	You know what it's got to do with me.

ADAM:	No. We're not exclusive.
STEPHEN:	But . . .
ADAM:	We have agreed.
STEPHEN:	Have we?
ADAM:	Didn't we?
STEPHEN:	Why didn't you tell me about him then?
ADAM:	I didn't want to rub your nose in it.
STEPHEN:	So he dumped you?
JANE:	Because you told him to.
STEPHEN:	Jane!
JANE:	Sad, isn't it? He followed you because you were cheating.
ADAM:	Cheating?
SAM:	Go Janey . . . Go Janey.
JANE:	He followed you and then threatened Sam with the only thing that really frightened him – being found.
ADAM:	I don't understand.
JANE:	He blackmailed Sam into dumping you.
ADAM:	Did Sam tell you that?
JANE:	No. He did.

ADAM: You blackmailed him?

STEPHEN: I just asked him. I didn't force him to do anything.

ADAM: You had no right.

STEPHEN: You knew it wasn't in the rules really. You wouldn't have hidden it from me if you weren't ashamed of it. It was for your own good.

ADAM: You had no right.

STEPHEN: What do you care anyway? It's not as if he meant anything to you. I mean, it was just sex, wasn't it? Why should you care if I did ask him not to see you any more? It was a financial relationship I assume?

ADAM: What relationship isn't?

STEPHEN: But I love you.

ADAM: So?

STEPHEN: It's got to mean something.

ADAM: I loved Sam. Didn't stop him leaving me, did it?

STEPHEN: You loved him?

SAM: (*Whispering in Jane's ear*) He loved me.

ADAM: Yes. That's something to be ashamed of, isn't it? Loving someone like Sam.

SAM: He loved me.

STEPHEN:	You couldn't.
ADAM:	What?
STEPHEN:	You loved him, but you won't love me.
ADAM:	Stop the car.
SAM:	He loved me.
STEPHEN:	You . . . you little bastard.
ADAM:	Stop the fucking car. And you . . . what's your name?
JANE:	Jane.
ADAM:	Jane, piss off!

SCENE 12

*Ruth is in the kitchen. **Rob** and **Bethan** enter.*

BETHAN: I'm really sorry, Ruth.

She hands over the car keys.

ROB: I'm calling the police.

*Rob exits. **Bethan** looks at the broken plates on the floor.*

RUTH: How could you leave her on her own?

BETHAN: I'm sorry.

RUTH: Don't you think it's about time you grew up?

BETHAN: What?

RUTH: Love isn't just hearts and flowers, you know. It's about taking responsibility for each other.

Rob comes back in holding a phone.

BETHAN: Mrs Souza, I . . .

ROB: Ruth.

RUTH: You want me to be fair?

                Everything's broken; broken in bits and dust everywhere.

ROB: You should go home. Your parents are going out of their minds.

BETHAN: Shit . . . you didn't tell them about Jane and me?

RUTH: I don't know what I said.

BETHAN: But you wouldn't.

RUTH: Wouldn't I?

BETHAN: But you shouldn't.

RUTH: Shouldn't be fucking my daughter.

BETHAN: I'm sorry . . . I . . .

ROB: Just go . . . she doesn't mean it . . . just go.

Bethan exits.

ROB: Ruth?

RUTH: Yeah. I'm a monster. Aren't I?

ROB: It's the stress.

RUTH: Bollocks.

ROB: He made you like this.

RUTH: No, darling. I was just as bad as he was.

ROB: But you left.

RUTH: Why do you think? Because I couldn't take it?

ROB: Because you were brave.

RUTH:	No. Because I knew I could've killed him . . . I stabbed him, and Jane saw me. I thought she was asleep.
	Five, she was.
ROB:	He beat you. Bullied you . . . mental . . .
RUTH:	Did you have a breakdown because you were bullied into doing things you hated or because you did them?
ROB:	I have changed.
RUTH:	What do you mean?
ROB:	I am not the person I was.
RUTH:	Right.
ROB:	Jesus.
RUTH:	What?
ROB:	I can't marry you.
RUTH:	What?
ROB:	You don't think I've changed. Do you?

SCENE 13

*Sam and **Jane** are walking back to where **Sam** died. It is night. **Sam** has a torch. He appears and disappears into the dark.*

JANE: It's so dark. Are we nearly there?

SAM   You're tired.

JANE: No. Is it far?

SAM: Listen to me. I was wrong. You don't want to go there.

JANE: I've got to.

SAM: You've been walking for hours. Rest.

JANE: I've got to find out what happened to you.

         Why can't you just tell me?

SAM: I bet those two are ripping bits out of each other by now.

JANE: It isn't funny. Keep moving.

SAM: Talk to me.

JANE: Got nothing to say.

SAM: You feel bad?

JANE: Did you love Adam?

SAM: I don't know.

JANE:	Would it have made any difference to you?
SAM:	No.
	Tell me a story.
JANE:	I've told enough stories. I just want to find out the truth.
SAM:	You didn't finish the story you were telling Bethan.
JANE:	I didn't think you liked it.
SAM:	What happened to the boy with a beautiful voice and a chest of feathers?
JANE:	I don't know.
SAM:	Come on. You can do better than that.
JANE:	He knew he had to leave. All right? But where would he go? How would he make his way in the world?
SAM:	All the money from those ladies.
JANE:	Exactly. He ran back to his room and collected up some of the fine gifts he'd been given by all those fine ladies. He tied them up in a bundle like Dick Whittington and left the chewing-gum pavements of London to travel the world.
SAM:	See, you can do it.
JANE:	Come on.
SAM:	Keep going.

JANE:	After many days he came to a great bridge. It was a fine bridge, so fine and bridgey. Its green structure reminded him of the copper spires of the churches in London. But as he strode across the bridge a great troll stirred beneath the silted waves. She was an ancient troll, as amorphous as a bag of mud, her breath as pungent as silage and she grew barnacles and oysters in her fanny.

Sam laughs.

SAM:	What did she say?

JANE:	She said, 'Who is this boy, with flaxen hair, lips of cherries and eyes of sky? Who is this boy who sings when he walks and charms my tired old boot of a brain? Who is this boy?'

SAM:	He said, ''Tis I, Samuel Clarke of Farringdon. I come to this country to find my fame and fortune!'

JANE:	And the old troll laughed and laughed and the sea welled up in great bubbles and swirls. 'Oh my dear, that's what they all say,' she said. 'Good luck, but if you sing me one more song I'll tell you what your fortune shall be.'
	And so he sang, he sang a sweet, sweet song and the old girl almost felt bad when she finally said, 'You are moving towards your destiny faster than you know.'
	'And what is my destiny?' he cried.
	'To be betrayed by the one who loves you most,' she replied.

SAM:	We're here.
	See that bridge? Over that, down onto the mud, out towards the sea, it's low tide again.

JANE:	What happened to you, Sam? Who took you away?
SAM:	Don't you know yet?
JANE:	NO!
SAM:	Come on, it's just us here now, you can tell me. Who did this? Who?
JANE:	I don't know.
SAM:	You do, you do know. Come on. Follow me. I'll show you.
JANE:	Wait, I can't see where you've gone.
SAM:	I'm here . . . right beside you.
JANE:	Where?

Sam comes back into the light.

SAM:	Here.
JANE:	Don't leave me.
SAM:	This is the very spot.
JANE:	There's nothing here, Sam.
SAM:	So?
JANE:	What?
SAM:	Who is?
JANE:	I can't see you.

SAM:	I'm right here.
JANE:	Stay. I don't understand.
SAM:	You know who did it.
	You've always known.
	Sad.
JANE:	I don't know.
SAM:	You do. Say it.
	Tell me, you stupid bitch.
	It was you.
JANE:	No.
SAM:	You killed me.
JANE:	No.
SAM:	Why are you still alive, Jane?
JANE:	But you . . . I've never been here before.
SAM:	You should have been with me. We planned it all. We were going to get the train out into a place where no one would find us. We saved the money.
JANE:	But I didn't mean –
SAM:	You gave it to me, I saved it.

JANE: But we never definitely decided when, did we?

SAM: You're a very good girl really, aren't you, going to college, doing your homework? OK, so you cut yourself a bit, but you always manage to make it to hospital, don't you? You always somehow manage to get better, you always get found at the last moment, don't you? Very convenient, that.

           I found you. Do you remember? I was the one who found you last year. I saved your life.

JANE: I know.

SAM: I got Bethan and we got you to hospital and told your Mum and Rob. We saved your life. Why did we do that?

           You didn't thank us. Did you? You just said you wanted to die.

JANE: I do. (*She is crying now*)

SAM: And it was your idea that we came out here, wasn't it? You said you didn't want to live and I agreed since we're best friends. We said we'd never be found. No one would find us out here. Would they? Not for fousands of years. But one of us just carried on cutting themselves and going to get the nice nurses to patch them up again. How many times, Jane?

           Here's your chance to do it properly. You killed me. Now it's your turn. Lie down.

JANE: What?

SAM: Lie down. This is where I lay. It's not so bad really. Come on, next to me. That's it. No one will rescue you out here.

SAM (con.):   Now put your arm like this and your foot, there . . . perfect. Now close your eyes. Just close your eyes and wait. The tide will come in and go out and come in again. We'll be together and I won't be lonely any more.

Sam and Jane lie down together.

SAM: That's it, close your eyes.

Jane is back up on her knees, pleading and digging into the mud.

JANE: No. No. No.

She grabs hold of him.

JANE: Don't leave me, don't leave me out here.

I don't want to die.

SCENE 14

Stephen finds Adam on the road.

STEPHEN: Come on, get in.

Adam gets in the car.

ADAM: Is it true?

STEPHEN: Yes.

ADAM: When?

STEPHEN: A month ago.

     How did he end it?

ADAM: Not telling you.

     Giving you the satisfaction.

STEPHEN: What satisfaction?

ADAM: You know.

     You used that girl.

STEPHEN: I was trying to help.

ADAM: So why did you tell her about me and Sam? Why tell her and not me?

STEPHEN: I'm going to end it. Now.

Stephen stops the car.

ADAM: What?

STEPHEN: I don't think we should see each other any more. I don't
             want this. I don't want to do this any more. To think what I've
             done . . . to follow someone, threaten them, it's wrong, I
             must have been mad. I don't want to be that . . . I'm too
             old to dislike myself this much.

ADAM: What's with all this 'wrong' all of a sudden?

STEPHEN: I should have helped Sam. I should have helped him even
             though he was taking you away from me.

ADAM: Very noble.

STEPHEN: You said you loved him, was that noble?

ADAM: I just did.

STEPHEN: Why? Why did you love him and not me?

ADAM: He was special.

STEPHEN: Why? Why was he so special?

ADAM: He was cute, he was streetwise.

STEPHEN: Just tell me the truth.

ADAM: He was cool.

STEPHEN: Try again.

ADAM: You wouldn't want me playing wifey . . . no, you love a bit

ADAM (con.):   of danger. But at the same time it's all very safe and respectable, or I was, until you found out that I was seeing someone else, someone like Sam.

STEPHEN: Don't be ridiculous.

ADAM: Suddenly you realise that someone isn't playing the same game.

STEPHEN: I'm not playing games.

ADAM: Yes, you are. You say you're leaving me, but you're not really, are you?

You just want to provoke me.

You want me to break down, confess my love, beg you not to leave.

STEPHEN: I don't want to play games.

ADAM: Please!

STEPHEN: Adam. I like playing games. But I like them indoors, with the rain outside against the windows. I like playing with someone I trust, from whom I have no secrets, other than maybe what I'm going to buy them for Christmas. I'm sure that sounds very boring to you, but this isn't exciting for me.

It's dull and empty.

ADAM: We said we'd have an open relationship.

STEPHEN: This isn't an open relationship. Open means honest, not shagging everything in south Wales with a pulse.

ADAM: I met Sam before I met you.

STEPHEN: So?

ADAM: He was the first man I slept with.

STEPHEN: What?

ADAM: When I started Uni.

STEPHEN: I thought . . . at school, at your boarder.

ADAM: I lied.

STEPHEN: I'm only the second.

ADAM: Basically.

STEPHEN: Why didn't you tell me?

ADAM: You wouldn't have wanted me.

STEPHEN: Yes, I would.

ADAM: I'm not stupid.

STEPHEN: Oh no. Me neither.

ADAM: I was in Cardiff for the day. Found a pub. I didn't know it was a gay pub. Just looked like a normal pub from the outside.

I don't know why I went into that grotty pub on that day, but he was there, sitting on his own as if he was waiting for me, as if it were preordained. We went to this house where he was staying on the sofa for a few nights while the guys were away and did it and did it until we could do it no more.

STEPHEN: And you say that you loved him?

ADAM: Yes. I did.

STEPHEN: That's just sex.

ADAM: He only had to touch my arm and my knees would shake. Why isn't that love? How could I want anything bad to happen to someone who made me feel like that? I wanted him to be healthy and happy so that he could keep making me feel that good. Why is that any different to what everyone calls love? You want to tie me up with love, never let me out of your sight. Maybe I loved Sam more than you think you love me. I let him be free. I wanted him to be happy. I let him go when he wanted to go.

STEPHEN: You didn't have a choice.

ADAM: He didn't dump me. He said he was leaving. He asked me if I wanted to go with him.

             I said no.

STEPHEN: Because of college?

ADAM: Hardly. I don't know what I'm doing there.

STEPHEN: So why didn't you go?

ADAM: You.

STEPHEN: Please.

ADAM: I loved Sam. But we couldn't live together. I couldn't make him happy. I couldn't bring him home to meet my parents.

ADAM (con.): He was a mess – homeless, uneducated, hopeless.

How can you love someone like that?

Stephen. I was ashamed of him, of myself. He disgusted me.

STEPHEN: But you loved him.

ADAM: When I was with him. When it was just the two of us, he wasn't hopeless, but in public he became someone else, people looked at me as if to say, 'Do you know him?'

I betrayed him.

STEPHEN: Oh Adam.

ADAM: I never lied to you.

STEPHEN: You never told me the truth either.

ADAM: I was just having fun. I didn't think that he was going to die.

STEPHEN: Was he suicidal?

ADAM: I don't know. What did he say when you told him to stop seeing me?

STEPHEN: He agreed straight away. I hardly needed to say anything. He just agreed. Then asked me if I could buy him a drink.

ADAM: Did you?

STEPHEN: He got pissed. I was going to let him sleep it off at home. Tell you everything. But then he just disappeared. Opened the car door and disappeared.

STEPHEN (con.): Went back to it all and that was the last time I saw him.

ADAM: What about us?

STEPHEN: I think we're quite a match.

ADAM: You wouldn't end up on a mud bank for anyone, would you?

STEPHEN: No. And neither would you.

ADAM: Let's go home.

STEPHEN: What about Jane?

ADAM: She could be anywhere by now.

STEPHEN: We can't just leave her out there.

ADAM: So tell the police . . . come on. Let's go . . . I'm starving.

SCENE 15

Jane, Stephen and Adam, Ruth and Rob are all on stage together although in different places. The light of dawn is beginning to break and the chorus of birds begins.

JANE: Sam. Sam. Listen. It's dawn.

She sits up.

JANE: It's beautiful. The sky is so beautiful. Can you see?

She turns. Sam isn't there any more. There is the body of a bird lying next to her. Carefully she scoops the bird up; kneeling, she holds it in front of her.

STEPHEN: A new day. Are you all right?

ADAM: It's almost like he never existed. Now that you know how I felt . . . it doesn't seem real any more. I feel sort of weightless.

STEPHEN: I hope Jane is all right.

Jane begins to dig a small grave for the bird.

JANE: There was once a strange boy with a beautiful voice but a chest of feathers. He moved to a new country where he began to feel himself changing. His whole body was aching. At first he thought it was all the travelling. But then one clear,

JANE (con.):   warm night he walked under a full moon and stars so clear that they marked out the depths of space. He came to a pool and decided to wash. He pulled off his clothes but just as he was about to step into the water he saw in that glassy surface not only his chest but his whole body was now covered with feathers, and not all of them were downy brown, there were larger ones; glossy white ones.

This was the second time his heart beat so fast and his stomach fluttered and his mind soared, but not for love. This time for fear. He dimly sensed what it meant as he dressed himself and pushed on through the new country.

I think it's deep enough now.

She puts the body in the hole.

RUTH: I can't stop thinking about Sam's parents.

ROB: It's dawn. Get some sleep. I'll wake you if there's any news.

RUTH: I'm sorry.

ROB: Yeah. OK.

JANE: After some time he came to a crossing. There was a girl there.

She went down one road but then came back and set off a few steps in the new direction, only to come back again.

'Come with me, I'll show you the way,' he said, and they set

JANE (con.): off together. They had many adventures and loved each other very much. Soon she longed to go back to that crossing and every day he talked less and sang more. They knew they had to part and so decided to go on one last adventure together. The girl went to get food for the journey, but as she came back she was waylaid by bandits. They left her black and blue by the side of the road so she couldn't get back to meet the waiting boy. He waited and waited while all the time she lay by the side of the road. After a while the boy remembered what the troll had said, 'You will be betrayed by the one who loves you most', and he thought, 'Jane loves me. I know, so now she has betrayed me. The old troll told the truth.' And with that he shut his eyes and leapt up into the sky. He stretched out his wide white wings and flew into the sky. For the third time his heart beat and his stomach fluttered and his mind soared, but not for love, and not for fear, but for joy, only joy.

She takes out the knife and puts it in the grave with the bird. She covers up the grave and exits. Lights out on **Stephen** *and* **Adam**.

RUTH: She's coming home.

ROB: Safe?

RUTH: Yes.

ROB: Good.

RUTH: Yes. It is good.

ROB: The police?

RUTH: Yes. They found her.

ROB:	Yes.
RUTH:	Good.
ROB:	Do you want a drink?
RUTH:	Yes.
ROB:	Yes. Me too.

SCENE 16

Jane is getting dressed for a party, she is wearing something light and cool. *Bethan is there.*

BETHAN: Suits you, that colour.

JANE: Yeah?

BETHAN: Yeah.

JANE: You look nice too.

BETHAN: Nice?

JANE: Rocking?

BETHAN: Very tidy in here.

JANE: We've been spring-cleaning.

BETHAN: Is that right?

            Looks good.

JANE: Look what we found.

Picks up a string of passport photos from somewhere it has been carefully stored.

BETHAN: God, look at my hair and Sam, oh, this was, this was my birthday, wasn't it?

JANE: Was it? I thought it was the last day of school.

BETHAN: No, it was my birthday and Sam took us to that party, you remember? It was all a bit Rocky Horror and then Mr O'Grady turned up in a dress. He saw us sitting on the staircase drinking vodka, just marched up to us, asked us what we thought we were doing. And Sam was like 'what are you doing, darling?' and we couldn't stop laughing, but then we had to go because everyone was looking at us.

JANE: Yeah, not embarrassing at all.

BETHAN: Come on, it was funny.

JANE: (*She goes and sits next to Bethan*) Yeah. I suppose. They're good photos.

Here. Have one. (*She tears one off*)

Thank you for coming. You do look really . . . fab.

BETHAN: That's OK.

JANE: Bethan?

BETHAN: Yes?

JANE: I want to say.

BETHAN: It's OK.

JANE: Bethan.

BETHAN: Don't. It's OK.

JANE: I'm sorry I haven't called.

BETHAN: Oh.

JANE:	You're not angry?
BETHAN:	I thought you were still angry with me.
JANE:	No. I wasn't angry with you.
BETHAN:	You told me to fuck off.
JANE:	I didn't mean it.
BETHAN:	Yes you did.
JANE:	Sorry.
BETHAN:	It's OK. You were a bit . . .
JANE:	Intense?
BETHAN:	Yeah, I suppose that's one way of looking at it.
	Oh. I've been going to this group thing.
JANE:	Group thing?
BETHAN:	Yeah, it's . . . it's like a club.
JANE:	Like a youth club?!
BETHAN:	Well, kinda. But it's OK. We're gonna go to London for the Mardi Gras with some other groups from Swansea and Bridgend and you know, it's all right. I've met some great people.
JANE:	You've met some great 'people'?
BETHAN:	Yeah.

JANE: Like girls?

BETHAN: I'm not seeing anyone special.

JANE: Oh, but you are seeing someone?

BETHAN: Not some *one* . . .

JANE: Aren't you the girl about town!

BETHAN: I'm just having fun.

JANE: I'm jealous.

            Had you all to myself for ages.

BETHAN: I didn't have you though.

            You do seem different.

            Do you feel different?

JANE: I've had my own group thing to do too, you know.

BETHAN: I know.

            Is it good?

JANE: It's not a social event.

BETHAN: I know.

            I mean. Is it good for you?

JANE: Yes.

JANE (con.):	I haven't cut for six months. Not once. I've wanted to but I haven't. It's going to get easier. I hope.
BETHAN:	I've missed you.
JANE:	Sounds like you haven't had time to miss me.
BETHAN:	Why don't you come with me one night?
JANE:	I could do.
BETHAN:	Yeah, course you could. You're not the only one, you know.
JANE:	What?
BETHAN:	You're not the only one who's been through this shit with doctors and hospitals and everything. I suppose I thought . . . I didn't understand, but quite a few of them have been through it too.
JANE:	Oh.
BETHAN:	Perhaps I was a bit hard on you?
JANE:	It's OK. It wouldn't have made any difference what you did.
BETHAN:	Really?
JANE:	Yeah.
	So what are your new girlfriends like?
BETHAN:	Nice.
JANE:	Nicer than me?

BETHAN:	Well . . .
JANE:	Well?
BETHAN:	Oh come on, you know.
JANE:	What?
BETHAN:	You're terrible!
JANE:	Why?
BETHAN:	You're trying to wrap me round your finger, like you always do.
JANE:	No I'm not.
BETHAN:	You tell me how you feel first.
JANE:	Well. I think I'm really sorry I told you to fuck off.
BETHAN:	And?
JANE:	And I still really like you.
BETHAN:	And . . .
JANE:	And I want to kiss you.
BETHAN:	Really?
JANE:	Really.
BETHAN:	Why?
JANE:	'Cause I think you're lush.

They kiss.

JANE: Hallo again.

BETHAN: Hallo.

                    Beautiful ceremony, wasn't it.

JANE: Beautiful.

They hug. Party music from the reception downstairs starts.

BETHAN: Sounds like the party's starting.

JANE: You've got to see Rob dancing.

BETHAN: Come on then. Is there something else?

JANE: Gonna save a dance for me?

BETHAN: Maybe.

THE END

With thanks to:

Angela
Helen
James
James
Pat
Tom
Valerie